# Ruled by Faith

James A. Galezewski

outskirts press

Outskirts Press, Inc.
http://www.outskirtspress.com

ISBN: 978-1-9772-4851-0




PRINTED IN THE UNITED STATES OF AMERICA

Dedicated to all of those men and women throughout history who had the courage to question conventional wisdom, the things everyone "knew" were true, and to search for better answers. They often paid a steep personal price for their audacity, while greatly advancing the cause of mankind.

# Table of Contents

# Preface

> Freethinkers are those who are willing to use their
> minds without prejudice and without fearing to
> understand things that clash with their own customs,
> privileges, or beliefs. This state of mind is not
> common, but it is essential for right thinking...
> — **Leo Tolstoy**

**SAUDI ARABIA'S CONSTITUTION** is the Qur'an and the Sunnah, which are the Islamic scripture and the body of traditional Islamic social and legal practices. The nation is an absolute monarchy. Corruption is widespread and dissent is not tolerated. Although the king and royal family are required to abide by the Qur'an, religious leaders pretty much leave them alone. For others, punishment is extreme and barbaric. Offenders may suffer public caning, amputation, stoning to death, or have an eye gouged out. The death sentence, usually carried out by public beheading after Friday prayers, may be imposed for various offenses, including "sorcery". Most people in modern societies are aghast at these practices. How could the Saudis be convinced to change their system? Their actions are based on their faith in what God (Allah) has commanded, and therefore believe they are righteous and just. The only way to convince them that their conclusion about what conduct to punish and how to sanction it is wrong, would be to first convince them that their premise, that they have a deity who requires or is pleased by such punishment, is wrong. That would be a formidable task, as it challenges the very foundation of their society, a society in which death is also the prescribed penalty for apostasy. In the unlikely event you were successful in your efforts, they would be left in a vacuum. If their culture, religion and justice system were eliminated, what would replace them?

It is no coincidence that the region of the world dubbed "The Holy Land" is one of the most hate-filled powder kegs on the face of the earth. It is a region with warring factions fighting over territory, each of which is convinced that their deity gave the territory to them and He requires they defend it for future generations. Just as in the Old Testament, both sides believe they have divine license to kill anyone who would take the land from them. There is no objective, reasonable way to put their heads together and determine which group the Almighty really wants to inhabit the land, or certain parts of it, or to determine how boundaries might be drawn. There is no evidence to substantiate either of the competing claims of God's favor, only unprovable and untestable assertions based on religious faith. Any compromise or settlement would amount to a denial of that faith and the divine charge to defend it.

While most Americans are astounded at the barbarism of Saudi Arabia, and the intractable violence of the Midler East, we don't have to look too far to see similar religious influences in America. Consider the following quote:"There are two nations created for God's glory – Israel and the United States of America. We stand strongly with Israel. We will not back down until we have everything God has promised us". Those words were spoken by a member of the United States Congress in 2021. We are special in God's eyes. He is on our side. We are a nation favored by God, and we always were. Coined in 1845, the term Manifest Destiny described a doctrine that America was a nation, destined by God, to expand Westward across North America from coast to coast. Since it was destined by God, we were justified in killing whoever stood in the way, and we did. In our own history, we also used religious justification for using fellow humans as chattel slaves, and burning the occasional witch at the stake as the need arose.

Cemeteries throughout the world are filled with the bodies of young soldiers who were convinced that their cause was just and they fought with divine blessing. Their bravery was emotionally fueled by flags, anthems, tribalism, and the belief that their mission was supported by God, as verified by their religious and military leaders. In the event they were killed, they would reap an eternal reward of happiness, glory, or willing virgins in Heaven, Valhalla (Norse), Elysium (Greek), The Field of Reeds (Egyptian), or wherever their particular religion taught them they would go. No doubt soldiers on both sides of a conflict wondered how their opponent could be so deluded as to believe God was on *their* side, when it is plain for any fool to see He is on *ours*.

It seems to be a common theme that nations use their might to wage wars when they have divine approval to do so. Yet competing factions can't both be killing each other on behalf of God – one side must have it wrong, and possibly both sides. Punishing the populace for wrongdoing and waging war are not the only ways societies are influenced by their religious beliefs. Even in modern America, religion percolates through every aspect of our society. I recently noted a program in Colorado in which teens received free birth control without parental approval, which resulted in a dramatic decrease in teen pregnancy, and abortions. The cost to the State was more than offset by savings in payments for labor and delivery, child care assistance and food stamps. I was asked why that wasn't widely known. My answer was that public policy decisions involving reproduction don't require data, facts or evidence. Belief in what heaven commands suffices for many of us. Recent political discourse in America has been filled with claims of who was told by God to run for public office, what legislation God supports, His view of homosexuality and abortion, and His preferred curriculum and practices in public schools. Even COVID vaccinations, which have become a political issue, are not exempt from such claims. I recently saw a social media post that aligned refusal to be vaccinated with God's will on the matter. The claim seems pretty absurd, but it does illustrate how divine authority is claimed by someone to support almost any political view there is.

When the outcomes of our laws and practices fall short, different approaches may produce better results. Often, the premise we relied on to fashion the law or practice was false. If our premise of divine direction and approval doesn't pan out, it could be due to a false premise – we didn't have the heavenly guidance and approval we thought we had. In that case, we would do well to backtrack and reconsider the validity of our premise. The decision to adopt religious belief is not just about the hereafter; it has immense consequences for our society and the world we live in as well. For that reason alone, the answer to the question of what is true about religious belief merits careful and thoughtful examination. I hope to offer such an examination here. Afterward, no matter your conclusion, we have to find a way for individuals and societies who have reached different conclusions to coexist peacefully and amicably.

The first and most important question to answer is whether there is a God. It is the most important, because if there is no God, all of the other arguments about His or Her wishes, characteristics, which sacred writings are genuine and how they should be interpreted, are meaningless. If we conclude there is a deity, the next questions to answer is which of the many thousands of deities mankind has worshipped throughout history is the right one, and what are this God's wishes? We should also consider the effects of religious belief, because religious faith has an impact on our lives and society. What people believe informs their decisions, regardless of whether or not the belief is true. We carry our beliefs with us into the voting booth, the jury room, and in raising our children. We should also consider how people think, develop their views, and hold onto ideas even when the facts and evidence don't support them. That awareness could lead us to be more tolerant of the views others hold, to hold our own beliefs more tentatively and perhaps give us some insight into how others might be persuaded.

After I wrote my first book I was told, with some merit, that I wrote too much about myself and my background. Still, I think the reader should know something about me and how my views were formed. To that end, I will mention that I was reared as a Roman Catholic, and attended Catholic schools through high school. In my experience, they had a way of filling children with a sense of guilt, even over things they had no control over. Maybe my prayer would have been answered or this terrible event wouldn't have happened, if I had been better, prayed more, or my faith was stronger. Somehow, I shared at least some degree of responsibility for nearly every bad event or outcome. In college, I became acquainted with Baptist and Pentecostal students, attended bible studies, and became familiar with their faith. I learned that professing to know things that nobody really can know with certainty demonstrates the strength of your faith. I learned that meeting regularly with other believers reinforces the faith you have chosen, and avoiding those who disagree minimizes the risk of losing that faith. I came to believe a lot of what was proclaimed in the realm of faith was really disingenuous. I was told that is why we need to keep our eyes on God, not the pastor, apologist or any individual. That calls to mind a line from the *Wizard of Oz,* "Pay no attention to the man behind the curtain". In the movie, as in religion, there was a reason to ignore the man behind the curtain; watching him leads you to discover the deception.

Eventually, I couldn't convince myself that those things I heard preached were true. I found some believers consider it a challenge to pretend to believe things that they knew were highly improbable, and overcoming that challenge was regarded an admirable accomplishment. Unlike them, I wanted to *know* what was true. Not what someone declared was true and I must believe "or else", not what was comforting or reassuring to believe, but what was in all likelihood, factual. So, I read books. Most importantly, my views were informed by books of fact, evidence and scholarship, not books of doctrine, personal relevation or spirituality.

The reader may know that Thomas Jefferson edited his own bible; one that kept the parts about Jesus' teachings, but edited out the miraculous events that he didn't believe really happened. To do that, he had to discard all the conventional thinking of his time and have the courage to search for what he really believed was the truth. Many are afraid to even entertain the possibility that ideas about religion that differ from what they were taught to believe as children could be correct. Those timid souls who are too afraid to wonder or question will never know, and will forever be haunted by their own doubts.

I have had enough discussions about religion with people to realize that trying to get someone to discuss it objectively is often an insurmountable challenge. Most people believe what they want to believe, what they were taught to believe, what other like-minded people in their social circle believe and what *feels* right to them. Challenges to their belief are often regarded as mockery or persecution. No evidence, no logic, no reason, will ever penetrate that armor. Like a toddler with a security blanket, even a slight tug at it produces an emotional reaction as they pull away and clutch it all the more tightly. Their responses use many different words, all of which really mean "that's not what I believe, not what I want to believe, and nothing you can say will change my mind". I did not write this book for them. I wrote it for the curious, the inquisitive, the people who ask "why?", "says who?", "how do they know?", and "are you sure?". I wrote it for people who are unafraid to question the wisdom of their culture, traditions, and the things "everybody knows" are true. To them I offer some ideas, some analysis and some evidence they may not have encountered before, that I hope will help them in their search for the truth. One day it will be they who find a better way for mankind to move forward and correct the mistakes of the past.

# CHAPTER 1

# The Case for God

The whole problem with the world is that fools
and fanatics are always so certain of themselves,
and wiser people so full of doubts.

— **Bertrand Russell**

**MOST PEOPLE AGREE** that in discussing an issue, the burden of proof rests on the party who put forth the proposition. So if you tell me there is a deity, it is up to you to prove it, not up to me to prove your claim is false. Without proof, the proposition fails and is rejected. That is the atheist position; you are claiming there is a God, you can't prove that, so I don't believe your assertion is true. Theists will sometimes try to flip the burden of proof onto the doubter; "I can't prove there is a God, but neither can you prove there isn't", thus implying the views are equally valid choices, both requiring a degree of faith. They are not. With that reasoning, one could assert any nonsense they wanted, such as alien abductions or Sasquatch, and if you couldn't prove it false, both views would be equally acceptable and valid. Belief in alien abductions or Sasquatch would be just as reasonable as disbelief. The lack of evidence to validate a particular belief as factual does not produce a tie with the skeptic who is unconvinced. Instead, it provides a valid basis for skepticism and disbelief. Unlike many other religions, Pastafarians, who belong to the church of the Flying Spaghetti Monster (FSM), are an open minded religion. They reject dogma and willingly admit their faith may not be true, if you can prove it is false. Of course, their faith is no more subject to being objectively proven or disproven than any other.

I once considered myself an agnostic with regard to religion. That was partly due to skepticism, and partly due to fear. Affirmatively asserting you don't believe in God, rather than just having doubts, takes you to a new level; one that differs from most of American society, the people in your social circle, and your family. Every religious person who is honest will tell you that they sometimes have doubts. Many people who admit they are not devout and rarely if ever attend church often add the disclaimer that they still believe in God. Atheism is a whole different animal than doubt or uncertainty. It crosses a line into disbelief and rejection of religion. Public sentiment toward atheists has changed very slowly and is generally intolerant. For example, it wasn't until 2008 that Parliament abolished the crime of blasphemy in England and Wales. Blasphemy remains a crime that is on the books in Scotland, though it hasn't been enforced in recent times.

Before writing this chapter, I saw a post on Facebook proclaiming "Jesus is the reason for the season", referring to the holiday season. Lots of old friends of mine liked or loved it. Not a single dissent. Never mind that New Years Day, Hanukkah and Kwanza have nothing to do with Jesus; Christmas is *our* favored holiday during the season and has a religious significance to *us*, which every right-thinking American should share. Never mind that we don't know when Jesus was really born, or that Christianity chose the time of the celebration to coincide with pagan holidays celebrating the winter solstice. The season existed long before Jesus, and celebrating it pre-dated Jesus by thousands of years, but the religious reason *we* celebrate is the *real* reason. Our understanding of history tends to revolve around our own culture and our own religious beliefs. Disagreement or skepticism is often met with something less than kindness. It's a little like being the only one to say the emperor isn't wearing any clothes, with the added threats of social ostracism and eternal damnation. So I needed to feel confident in it before asserting my skepticism to others.

Christianity argues that there must be a God. Assume for the sake of argument they could prove that position is true; that there must be something, some being with a higher power, responsible for us and for all of creation. If we accept that there must have been a deity responsible for creation, how do you know that deity was immortal, and that He didn't die two weeks after creation? How do you know it was the Christian deity who is responsible and not some other? How do you know the deity that created everything is involved in the world today, cares about us, answers prayer, or provides us with an afterlife? There are a lot of questions to answer, and the existence of a deity is just the beginning. Let's start at the beginning then, and examine the case for and against the existence of a God.

**Ex Nihilio**: Literally, "out of nothing" in Latin. The argument is that the universe; space, time, and matter, exist. Everything we know of comes from something. Children come from parents. Trees come from seeds. Islands come from volcanoes. Follow the chain of causes back to the beginning of the universe. What is the first cause? What or who, was not created and had no beginning? Their answer, of course, is God. I might ask if everything has a cause, who created God? Their answer is God always existed and had no cause. We could agree then, that something or someone had to exist without a creator or a cause. How do you know that the energy that fueled the Big Bang didn't always exist and had no cause? You don't. In fact, it's a better hypothesis than God, because we know with certainty that energy exists, and we know from physics that energy can't be created or destroyed, only transformed. The believer is just adding a deity as another layer on top of the chain of causes. When the believer gets to the top of the chain of causes and doesn't know what came before, they throw God on the top. In that case, God is little more than a convenient word used to explain the unknown.

That is sometimes called the God of the Gaps. Any gap in mankind's knowledge is explained by "God". As our knowledge of physics, biology, and other sciences has grown in modern times, the number of gaps filled by God keeps getting smaller. Our expanding knowledge allows us to explain more and more of the universe and how it works without God or any other supernatural power. The Bubonic plague is no longer caused by God as punishment for sin; it's caused by the bacterium Yersinia pestis that is transmitted from rats to humans through flea bites. Earthquakes are not caused by a deity's anger at something we did or failed to do, but by movement of the tectonic plates under the earth's surface. God, until you can prove His or Her existence, isn't an answer to any question. God is just a bookmark that holds a place of uncertainty until the answer is discovered; an unproven supposition that takes the place of "I don't know", until we do know. Some of us feel comfortable in a world in which we don't, and may never, know everything. Those who need an answer to everything right now often resort to God as an explanation.

**Argument from Design / Teleological Argument**: The argument in brief, is that the universe is so finely tuned, that there must have been a being who designed it. It's difficult to imagine how all of the pieces of our world work together without also imagining a creator who created and assembled all the pieces, and the rules by which they operate.

If those rules were ever so slightly different, mankind would not even exist. Proponents of this view have long used the watchmaker analogy. If you are walking on the beach and find a watch, you know that it was not simply made and deposited there by the forces of nature. Watches require sophisticated design which makes it obvious there must have been a watchmaker. So too, when we see all of the complexity of the universe, we know there must have been a creator.

There are also many counter arguments. If all of the vastness of the universe was created just to support the existence of a few creatures, on one planet, in one solar system of a single galaxy, who have only existed for a very small fraction of the time the universe has been in existence, it would be a very wasteful design. Certainly an intelligent design would be an efficient design. Consider that only a small fraction of the earth itself is habitable by humans, making the earth itself inefficiently designed, if it was indeed designed for mankind.

Roman Catholics have an annual ritual in which the throats of the faithful are blessed. This ritual commemorates St. Blaise, a fourth century bishop who reportedly saved a boy who nearly died because of a fish bone in his throat. This would all be unnecessary if we were intelligently designed. Why do we eat and breathe through the same opening, thereby insuring thousands of people will choke to death every year? After all, other creatures, such as dolphins, have two separate openings; one for breathing and another for eating. Some have also pointed to vestigial organs, male nipples, the appendix and the human eye as evidence that human beings were not designed intelligently.

Another challenge to the argument for a designer is that the process of natural selection results in organisms adapting to their environment. Thus, finding life well suited to its environment is evidence of life's adaptation to the environment, not of an environment designed for the life in it. Those life forms that failed to adequately adapt to the environment became extinct, and those that remain fit their environment like a glove. In fact, of all the species that have ever lived on earth, 99% are extinct. They hit an evolutionary dead end and no longer exist. Would an intelligent designer create a broad array of life forms that were destined for extinction?

Darwin himself noted that *"If it could be demonstrated that any complex organ existed which could not possibly have been formed by numerous, successive, slight modifications, my theory would absolutely break down."* That challenge was taken up by Michale Behe, who argued for "irreducible complexity". That is, in a complex system, the removal of any one part destroys the functioning of the entire system, which is evidence that it could not have evolved. Though creationists seized on the idea, it mistakenly relies on the assumption that evolution only improves existing functions, when adaptation can produce changes in function. For that reason, biologists have pretty decisively rejected the Behe's hypothesis.

**Pascal's Wager**: This is an argument that we can't know for certain whether or not God exists, but we must make a bet one way or the other. Considering what we stand to gain or lose with either bet, the prudent wager is to bet there is a deity. Of course, this just suggests the best way to bet, and contributes nothing to the discussion of which alternative is actually true. Another critique is that an omniscient God would certainly discern and not credit a profession of belief that was not genuine, and only claimed out of fear of the potential consequences.

**The Problem of Evil**: This is sometimes similarly argued as the problem of suffering. My dad was in Patton's Third Army during WWII. He once told me that he was required to tour the first concentration camp that was liberated, where he saw bodies "stacked up like cordwood". On another occasion, he told me that he sometimes wondered how God could have ignored the cries and prayers of millions of innocent people, begging and pleading for His help and mercy, as they were being starved, abused and slaughtered. That in essence is the problem of evil. The Greek philosopher Epicurus raised the question centuries before the birth of Jesus. *Is God willing to prevent evil but not able? Then He is not omnipotent. Is He able but not willing? Then He is malevolent. Is He both able and willing? Then whence comes evil? Is He neither able nor willing? Then why call Him God?* If God is omnipotent, then evil can only exist because He allows it and chooses not to stop it.

Some prominent atheists turned to atheism because they found no satisfactory resolution to this problem. How can a kind and loving God fail to protect children from sexual abuse by clergy in his own church? Because it would interfere with the abuser's free will? If you knew a child was being abused and you were able to stop it, wouldn't you? Of course you would. I spent a career in policing that entailed interfering with the free will of evil men. Would God do less? So it seems. There are thousands of innocent children dying of starvation and disease every day. Innocent people die by the hundreds of thousands in tsunamis and other natural disasters. How can this kind, omnipotent and loving God permit it? Some answers are, "we don't understand Gods ways", "We are not to question him", "Bad men have free will", "It's a mystery", and of course, "Satan". I would remind these apologists of their own scripture, Isaiah 45:7. The God you worship created good and evil, free will, Satan, bad men, and the environment that is so often hostile to human life. He could have created it (and us) in a way that did not require such misery.

Consider the fate of wild animals that, in the natural order of such things, often die a horrible and painful death being torn apart and eaten alive by predators. What harm have they caused to deserve that fate, what sin have they committed, and what reward awaits them for their suffering? What is the purpose of designing such suffering into the way the world works? The deity who created this is either not kind, loving, and compassionate as we have been taught, is not omnipotent and can't intervene, or even more plausible, doesn't't exist at all.

I recently saw a theological argument that originated with St. Augustine put forward by a bishop; when God allows something evil or bad to happen, it occurs so that something better or greater can happen. The example he cited is the mighty lion. The gazelle dies, so that the mighty, noble lion, something greater, can survive. Such arguments belie the problem with philosophical arguments in general that the religious often rely on. What makes the lion better, more noble, glorious or superior to the gazelle? Without any evidence for that underlying assumption, why are we to accept the assumption as true? Further, the argument ignores the fact that God could have created a world, if He so chose, without the need for the lion to eat the gazelle, a world in which the suffering was not necessary. We are left to wonder what the greater good might be when a child is molested by an adult they trusted. The religious often claim that God's ways are beyond our understanding. It would be far more accurate to say that their claim of what His ways are is what is beyond understanding and simply doesn't make sense.

Apologists sometimes put forward the argument that the world was created to be perfect and free of suffering and was, up until Adam and Eve and their fall. I will discuss Genesis later and the evidence that it is little more than folklore. However, even if you accept it, you are left to explain why, thousands of years later, people and even animals who had no role in the fall should be punished for the decision of one couple in antiquity. You also have to explain why a loving deity would intentionally and knowingly create such defective beings, such that His justice would compel Him to torment them and their offspring for all of their lives. An omniscient deity would have known about Adam's fall before it occurred and yet He went ahead with that plan anyway. He could have created them without the defects that produced that necessity of punishment. Either the story is not true, God doesn't have the characteristics Christians ascribe to Him, or the story is not true *and* there is no deity with the characteristics they describe.

Since free will is linked closely to the problem of evil as well as many philosophical and theological positions, it merits some consideration at this point. Free will is a theoretical belief that helps explain away the cruelty and suffering that is a fact of life for all living beings. We subscribe to it intuitively, because when we make a choice, it feels like we could have chosen any of the options that were available. There is compelling evidence that points to the fact that you may have been cognizant of the other options and felt you could have chosen any of them, but you chose the option you were most strongly influenced to choose. Our choices are anything but free. Following are a few observations that call our freedom of choice into question.

- A person who is hungry chooses what to eat. The choice they made was limited by their finances. Perhaps steak or lobster was out of the question because of the cost. They could have stolen the more expensive food, but were socialized to believe that such theft was wrong and the subsequent guilt would have outweighed the enjoyment, especially if there were other options available. Their choice of food was heavily influenced by the food prevalent in their culture. If born in America, they probably didn't choose to eat a bowl of rice, a guinea pig, or an insect, all staples in other cultures. In a few limited circumstances, nutritional needs may dictate a food choice, as when someone has a pica, or when a sodium deficiency causes them to choose something with a high salt content. Women are twice as likely to experience food cravings as men, and are more likely to crave sweet foods, while men are more likely to crave savory foods, so gender plays a role in the choice, even if the choice felt completely free. People experiencing a negative mood are more likely to crave "comfort food". Your brain may have come to associate certain foods with certain contexts, as when you choose popcorn in a movie theatre or fish on a Friday during Lent. You are more likely to select food that tastes good to you, which depends on your individual taste buds. In turn, your taste buds sensitivity to certain tastes is affected by your genes, gestation, hormones and thyroid. Certain medical conditions can also change food preferences, including diabetes, dementia, and Parkinson's disease. While one may feel they freely chose what to eat, the choice was actually the result many influences the person was not even consciously aware of.

- Studies in neuroscience have shown us that choices are made in deeper, unconscious regions of our brain and transmitted to our consciousness. In other words, the decision was reached at a moment when their conscious brain was unaware of the choice and when, if asked, the person would tell us they were still free to make any choice they wanted. This alone is powerful evidence that our choices are determined by circumstances and events we are unaware of, and that the freedom we experience is illusory.

- We know of conditions in which behavior is not freely chosen. The obsessive compulsive doesn't freely choose to wash his hands over and over again, he is compelled to. The person with Tourette's syndrome doesn't freely choose to shout out something inappropriate, he is compelled to. The addict does not freely decide to continue using drugs, he or she has a craving that compels them, a craving that you lack and which makes their choice puzzling and perhaps incomprehensible to you. These behaviors are all compelled by the biology and chemistry of the brain, and are not freely chosen.

- In 1966, Charles Whitman knew something was very wrong with him. He saw a both a physician and a psychiatrist hoping to find help. He felt a rage and a compulsion to kill, and didn't know why. He knew what the outcome would be and left behind a request for an autopsy after his death, suspecting there was something wrong with his brain that they might find. After killing his wife and mother, who he professed to love, he took up a sniper position with a rifle at the University of Texas, and became a notorious mass murderer before being killed by police. The source of his compulsion was found in the subsequent autopsy. He had a brain tumor. His behavior was compelled by the biology and chemistry of his brain. He behaved in a way he did not want to and that was actually contrary to his will.

- Any social worker, police officer, firefighter, nurse, teacher or probation officer in America could tell you a heart breaking story of children who never had a chance. Starting with poor prenatal care, poor nutrition, inadequate medical care, perhaps lead exposure, moving on to insufficient parental guidance, abuse, neglect, and poor education. Then put them in a segregated neighborhood filled with gangs, drug dealers and constant exposure to violence. Why does their free will lead to anti-social behavior, prison, and early death so much more often than the free will of their more privileged cohorts? Because it isn't about their free will. They follow the path that was laid out before them. True, sometimes kids rise above their circumstances, but they don't just wake up one day and freely decide on a different course out of the blue. I once heard a children's court judge say that for every one of those underprivileged kids who succeeded, there was a "someone" in their life. A parent, mentor, a teacher, coach, uncle, big brother, someone with whom they had a meaningful relationship and who guided, directed and inspired them, who showed them another path. He was right. That's exactly why mentoring programs have a track record of success. I would add that having a "someone" is not a choice the child made. A psychiatrist once joked that is precisely why he advises every child to be very careful in their selection of parents.

**Ontological Arguments**: This approach was started by St. Anselm in the 11th century, and has been tormenting undergraduate philosophy students ever since. It is an effort to reason your way to a God, without adding any actual evidence to the conversation. Therein lies the heart of its inadequacy. At one time, the arguments that made the most sense, that were most logical and reasonable, "proved" that the earth was flat and that the sun moved around it, when in fact, nobody knew. What logically seems to make sense is a poor way to explain the unknown. It makes absolutely no sense that subatomic particles randomly come into and out of existence, but they do. It defies common sense to assert that time itself did not exist before the Big Bang, but it didn't. It is impossible to use philosophy and logic to reason your way to those conclusions without empirical evidence. Knowledge of the unknown is acquired through repeated observation (whether direct or indirect), experimentation and testing, not through argument. At best, philosophical arguments provide a plausible hypothesis and train individuals in critical thinking skills; at worst, they provide confidence that falsehoods are factual, so that further study and research are unnecessary.

St. Anselm believed it is possible to imagine the greatest, most perfect of all possible beings. If you merely imagined it, it wouldn't be the greatest and most perfect, because it would be possible to imagine another that actually did exist, which would make it greater and more perfect than the one that didn't exist. Therefore, the greatest and most perfect being (God) must exist. It kind of hurts the brain to think about that argument, doesn't it? Of course, you could use that argument to "prove" anything exists, such as the perfect island.

A valid argument requires that the premises be true, and if they are true, the conclusion that follows from them must also be true. The challenge has been meeting both of those conditions; true premises and the conclusion they seek inevitably following from the premises. Ontological arguments have been refuted and refined by philosophers for a thousand years. In that time, nobody on either side of the debate has been declared the winner. The ultimate result of this exercise is that philosophers have something to write and teach about, thereby insuring the continued employment of philosophers. That is a great outcome for philosophers, but is largely a waste of time and energy for everyone else.

I lost my patience with philosophical musings in a college philosophy class when I was 18 or 19 years old. The professor was discussing cause and effect, and how we don't really see causes, and so don't really know the cause of an event. We just see a temporal sequence of two events, one that seems to follow the other, as when a pool cue hits a cue ball, and the ball propels forward. We don't really know one event caused the other, that the cue caused the ball to propel forward. I pointed out that if someone really believed that one event had no causal relationship to the other, they would be unlikely to survive for long in the real world. For example, there would be no reason for such a philosopher to believe that stepping out into the street and getting struck by a car is what caused the pedestrian's death. So just run out there. You don't really know the impact with the car caused the death.

I understand that the cause is inferred rather than seen directly, but it struck me as a silly waste of time to seriously discuss such notions.

**Moral Argument:** The moral argument notes that people across cultures and societies have a sense of ethics and morality. They argue we would not expect morality from a ruthless, selfish creature whose only purpose is to survive and reproduce. Either their morality is subjective, making it meaningless, or it is grounded in a moral law giver, God.

The question of whether morality is subjective or objective and whether that matters will be considered in chapter 5. For now, I will limit consideration of the moral argument to whether human morality is based on laws provided by God.

If the moral argument were true, one would expect that morality would be universally agreed upon. Yet we find a lack of agreement on what is moral across different cultures, religions, and even between different sects of the same religion. Why would a law-giver provide us with different laws to follow? Consequently, there is little reason to believe that we all have a universal moral compass that was somehow implanted in all of us by a supreme being. The argument also ignores the possibility, and I would argue likelihood, that our survival and reproduction are actually better served by adhering to certain standards of conduct in society.

A far more plausible explanation of morality is that humans evolved to be social animals, and have discovered that we can survive more effectively by banding together in groups. Living in groups facilitates tasks such as building, that require many hours of labor and a variety of skills. It also allows us to fight common enemies; wild animals, marauders, and other threats to us and our offspring, more effectively than we could as lone individuals. Just imagine how effective a lone individual would be in defending his homestead against an invading army. Unless this occurred in the context of a Rambo movie, the outcome is a foregone conclusion. However, banding together requires that we establish some ground rules so we can get along together. Stealing my property, cheating me in trade or raping my wife, are behaviors that are not conducive to social harmony. So, we made rules that members of our group had to follow, and sanctioned people who violated them. Now maybe some ancient, superstitious people had leaders who told them the rules came from the volcano god, the thunder god, or some other higher power they feared. That approach would certainly carry more weight than a mere pronouncement of "Here's how I think we need to behave as a group in order to get along". It might even get them to comply when nobody was around to enforce the rules. During the holiday season, I overheard my then 6 year old grandson explain to his younger sister, that "God and Santa Claus are watching you all the time". Constant, invisible surveillance with unavoidable consequences tends to increase compliance, as every parent knows.

**Personal Revelation and Experience**: Many people have claimed they know God exists, because He has revealed Himself to them or they have experienced His presence. That may take the form of a vision, but more often as a feeling, perhaps thoughts or dreams people have that they believe were given to them by God. It is impossible to objectively verify whether someone had a personal revelation, or whether their vision, thought or feeling actually came from a divine source. In evaluating the validity of such religious claims, it is appropriate to consider other things we do objectively know about these, and similar claims.

First, people have claimed many kinds of personal revelations and experiences that most of us have never shared, and are unlikely to have occurred. We know that many responsible, seemingly normal people have reported encountering UFOs and being abducted by aliens. We know that people who had near death experiences reported hovering above their bodies and watching the resuscitation efforts. We also know that when researchers arranged hospital rooms with pictures or symbols that could only be viewed by someone who was hovering above the bed, they failed to verify this phenomenon occurred among resuscitated patients in six separate research studies. We know that people can experience hallucinations caused by drugs, mental illness, sleep deprivation, and certain medical conditions that affect their brain function. The individual sincerely believes their experience was real, but it can't be verified objectively. So it is safe to say that an individual report of an event outside our normal experience is a poor source of evidence to rely on without reliable corroboration.

Second, it is curious who deities choose to communicate with. For example, Jesus generally doesn't seem to communicate with, guide, or direct anyone who is not already a fan. If he does, he apparently does it without attribution. Typically, it is Christians who get messages from Jesus. People of all faiths or no faith may get insights or new ideas about past events or their best future course, but it is usually attributed to Jesus only by people who already believe in Him. Without such faith, your idea may be an epiphany, an "aha" moment, or a message from a spiritual being you do believe in.

In Greece, I once took a tour of an ancient temple, dedicated to the goddess Athena. People of that time would come with questions for the goddess, which a male priest would relay to a priestess, who was in an underground chamber that contained methane gas. In her delirious state, she received an answer from the goddess which she relayed to a male priest, who in turn told the person who had asked. The answer never came from any of the other Greek gods, just the one that temple was dedicated to, and who was expected to provide an answer.

Interestingly, the answers were always vague and required the recipient to interpret them. Thus, the answer was never wrong, but the interpretation of it could be. Catholics, who revere her, seem to be the primary receivers of messages from the Virgin Mary. Pentecostals are reached by the Holy Spirit. Your idea may have even been given to you by a deceased relative, but only if you already believe deceased relatives are capable of such feats. Revelations are usually attributed only to sources that the receiver already believed in. That alone is good reason to be skeptical of the true source of these "revelations".

When I write, I become pretty immersed in the topic. Often, in the time between wakefulness and sleep, my mind wanders, and I will get an idea, sometimes several, to write about or incorporate into what I have already written. Knowing this, I keep a pen and notepad handy, lest I forget the idea before morning. It is a lot like brainstorming, but doing it alone; letting ideas flow without critical evaluation. We sometimes get ideas and have no inkling where they came from. You may have seen interviews with musical artists who got an idea for a song, wrote the music and lyrics in 20 minutes, and produced a huge hit. That's just how our brains work. The only difference is some people attribute the new idea to an agent, a separate being who "gave" it to them, to explain the experience. When you have the need of such an agent to explain your thoughts, the nature of the phenomena requires that the agent be unseen and spiritual. People naturally attribute it to the unseen spiritual agent they already believe in.

I once heard Bill O'Reilly describe how ideas came to him when he was writing in a manner very similar to my own experience. He attributed his to the Holy Spirit. When the interviewer expressed skepticism of that claim, O'Reilly accused him of "mocking my faith", as if his claim were itself sacred, and beyond questioning. Your book isn't just your thoughts ideas and research, but was inspired by the Holy Spirit?

The same way the Bible was inspired? I too would challenge him to prove it. If he can't, and there is no doubt he can't, we are rightly skeptical of his claim.

Third, consider how the significance of a statement changes if it was given to me by God, instead of just being my own idea. It becomes more credible. It comes from authority, and your compliance or non compliance with it can have consequences. You might even be more inclined to buy a book in which divinely inspired ideas were shared. If an idea came from God, there is no logical or reasonable argument you could put forward in opposition to it. People sometimes falsely use that claim of divine inspiration precisely for the weight it carries. Joseph Smith, the founder of Mormonism, was a convicted con man prior to revealing that which God showed only to him, and which provided the basis for that faith.

Oral Roberts, a Christian faith healer, once told his followers that God revealed to him that if he did not raise $8 million by the end of the year (1986), that he would die. Still short of the goal in January of 1987, he told a television audience that God would call him home, i.e. end his life, if he didn't raise the money by March. Apparently God's deadlines were somewhat flexible. Convinced of the certainty of the prophecy, his followers dug deep, met the goal, and the preacher was miraculously spared, just as God had promised. So it is pretty apparent to most of us who have not suspended our critical thinking about such matters, that the claim of a personal divine revelation is sometimes used deliberately for personal gain or to manipulate others.

In America, many have claimed that they were told or led by God to run for president; Herman Cain, Rick Santorum, Mike Huckabee, Ben Carson, John Kasich, Rick Perry, Scott Walker, Ted Cruz and Michelle Bachmann, to name a few. God even hedged His bet by encouraging multiple candidates to run against each other. Yet they all lost. One would do well to wonder why God would "tell" someone to run for office and then let them lose the election. These claims of divine guidance may or may not be deliberate misrepresentations. It is entirely possible that some individuals felt so strongly that it was the right decision, that they believed it must have been God leading them to it. Still, it has been observed that the decisions and actions the religious feel led to by God, usually coincide closely with their own goals, desires, and ambitions.

Reggie White was an exceptional defensive football player as well as an ordained evangelical minister. He was a dubbed "The Minister of Defense", incorporating both his football talent and his faith into one title. When he became a free agent, he signed a contract with the Green Bay Packers. He remarked at the time that he felt God led him to play in Green Bay. They also happened to be the team that gave him the best offer. A fortunate coincidence, no doubt. Perhaps, as many Wisconsinites seem to believe, God really is a Packer fan. Granted, He took a couple decades off in the 1970's and 1980's, but that was probably so we would really appreciate the team's success in later years.

Lastly, consider that psychologists have been able to recreate the emotionally overwhelming feeling of unconditional love that some interpret as experiencing God, without any reference to a deity at all. They used only an understanding of such emotions can be elicited. Even without such a sophisticated understanding of psychology, it is easy to stir emotions by using music. Hollywood learned long ago how to use musical scores to help stir the emotions of movie goers in sync with the story line. Music touches us at a very primal, emotional level. Whether it is the National Anthem, songs from your high school years, *How Great Thou Art* or *Amazing Grace*, there is likely music that touches you deeply. Different kinds of music can brighten your mood when you are down, calm you when you are agitated, or liven up a crowd. It is no coincidence that churches use music extensively. I remember hearing the pipe organ in church stop suddenly at the end of a song and feeling the vibrations as the last notes echoed through the church. It was powerful and awe inspiring, particularly so because of the acoustics of a large church. Whatever you consider the purpose of that music to be, it does touch many people at a deeply emotional level, and it works. How would a believer know if they were touched or moved by God, or by the music about God that was played in church? Feelings are subjective, and their cause can be ambiguous and hard to decipher. The emotions are genuine, but their divine attribution is dubious at best.

For these reasons, the personal experiences and revelation that some people offer as proof of God may feel real and compelling to them, but are of highly questionable validity. Even if they were completely valid, the subjective nature of a personal experience is not persuasive to others who have not shared that same experience. I find that a good rule of thumb to use when considering these and similar claims, is to ask if they can be falsified. Is there any way to test the claim and prove it is false? When it would be impossible to prove that a claim is false, treating the claim with skepticism is usually the best course.

**Nature**: Most of us have probably looked up into the sky on a starry night and felt a sense of awe and wonder. We may have been amazed at the beauty of a sunset, a rainbow, or a particular setting in nature. Many of us have marveled at the power of nature, making us feel small, weak and insignificant. You may have shared that sense when watching large waves crash into shore on a windy day, in a thunderstorm, a tornado, or some other natural event. The claim has been made that these things are all proof of God's existence (Romans 1:20). What is missing in this argument is a logical connection between the event or observation, and God.

There is no doubt that there are things in this universe that are awe inspiring, that there are powerful physical forces whose fury any of us would be helpless against, and there are many things that we don't understand. That proves humans experience awe, that human life is fragile, nature is powerful, and that there are things we don't know. What it doesn't prove, is that there is an invisible being in the sky who created and controls all the things that are powerful, beautiful, or beyond our understanding. Without providing a logical connection between them, apologists can only claim it is self-evident. My response is, "not to me". If one accepts this argument, I could similarly argue with equal validity, that my television is proof of the Flying Spaghetti Monster (FSM), and though you may not see how one is proof of the other, it is self-evident...except perhaps, to those who are blind and will not see.

# CHAPTER 2

# Choosing Your Deity

"Gods are fragile things; they may be killed by a
whiff of science or a dose of common sense."
— **Chapman Cohen**

**LET'S SAY THAT** you are persuaded that there must be a God. You really do, want to, or feel you must believe in a deity. Fair enough. People have worshipped, beseeched, honored and made sacrifices to thousands of different gods in the history of mankind. Deities give us some sense of control over events that are otherwise beyond our control, give us hope, inspiration, assuage our fear of death and give us answers where otherwise there would be none. How do you then determine which of them is (are) the real God(s) and distinguish them from the ones that are only myths and legends? If you are like most believers, you probably made a choice without giving this question much thought.

First, a lot of the deities of the past just fell out of favor. As far as I know, nobody ever proved Baal or Thor didn't exist. As cultures, civilizations and regions were conquered, changed and evolved, certain deities fell in favor and others out of favor. There are no temples to Baal or Thor in modern America, so worshipping them, and asking for their intercession probably never even occurred to you. That's how gods die. Nobody proves they don't exist and convinces the ignorant. Civilizations are conquered and assimilated, the deities once worshipped just quietly slip away, and new ones come along, often incorporating some of the attributes and powers of the old gods. Supernatural beings are artifacts of a culture, and they rise, fall and evolve with the culture they are a part of.

Accordingly, we can safely say that the deities of ancient civilizations that are no longer worshipped in the modern world are not under serious consideration. Of those remaining, how do people choose from among the available religious options? In ancient times, one way was to pray or make sacrifices to a deity asking for success in battle. If you later won that battle, it was evidence that the deity you asked was more powerful than the one(s) your enemy turned to, and more powerful than the god(s) who let you down in the past. If you later lost a battle, it could only be because you or your people somehow displeased Him and lost His favor. That method worked for the ancient Jews, all the way up to Constantine. In fact, Constantine's victory in one battle caused Christianity to soar in popularity and likely prevented it from ending the same way belief in Apollonius, another first century preacher / deity, ended.

In more recent times, deities are usually chosen differently. Look around, and the method should be apparent. Allow me to share the experiences that made it apparent to me. I grew up in a middle class Polish neighborhood. There was a smattering of other, mostly white nationalities, but it was largely a Polish neighborhood. Catholicism went hand in hand with being Polish. The two were interwoven with the culture. European boundaries changed, and at one point, there was no Poland at all, but the church, language and culture remained. My family attended a Polish parish named for a Polish saint with Polish priests who were bilingual, heard confessions in Polish as well as English, and sometimes gave sermons in Polish. Polish nuns taught in the parish school. There was a ritual involving the church to mark nearly every milestone of life; birth (baptism), reaching adulthood (confirmation, in which you affirmed your faith as an adult), marriage, a blessing for your new home, facing serious illness (sacrament of the sick) and death (requiem mass and funeral). You could even have your new car blessed by a priest. Many businesses were closed on Sundays, keeping holy the Lord's Day. Some had window signs that read "Closed Sunday, See you in church", telling you both the owner's religious observance, and what the owner thought your religious observance should be. There were various fasting and eating rules, Christmas customs (oplatki), chalk inscriptions above your door marking the feast of the 3 kings, Easter customs and much more.

Your identity as a person was interwoven with the foods, traditions, church, nationality and neighborhood of your youth. To leave the church would also be to leave your family, friends, culture, neighborhood, and identity behind, or at least loosen your ties to them. That would often be a huge and very uncomfortable leap to make. That is true of other religions and cultures as well. Depending on the faith you left, you might have some awkward encounters, hear some unpleasant remarks, be shunned and ostracized by the entire community including your own family, or worse. Islam teaches the appropriate penalty for apostasy is death. I have heard clergy refer to people who left and later returned to the church as "coming home". In a very real sense, they are returning home; returning to their roots, the people, the culture and traditions they were reared in.

Some years later in another neighborhood, I witnessed the sale of an unused public school to an Islamic group. They developed a mosque, a school and a community center that grew and expanded over several decades. Increasingly, Muslims were drawn to the neighborhood by the proximity of the development. Slowly over time, the neighborhood became more and more homogenous. Homes sold quickly at a good price, sparked by the surge in demand. Muslims wanted to live close to the mosque and its school, as well as other like-minded people who shared their culture and faith. The experience of Muslim children growing up in that environment must be similar to my own in many respects. Religious belief and culture intertwined, shared by relatives and neighbors, reinforced in school and in religious services, all carried out in a community of like-minded individuals.

My experience and observation is not unique to my hometown. Look around at the rest of the world. There is a direct correlation between geography and religion. If you were born in America, you are probably a Christian. You might later move to a different sect, but it is very unlikely you would convert to Islam or Buddhism. If you are Hindu, you likely have roots in India. If you were born in Iraq, you are probably Muslim. Southeast Asians are likely Buddhist. If you grew up in Utah, there's a good chance you are a Mormon. If you have a religious faith, it is probably the one you were taught to believe as a child. The one your parents and grandparents believed, the one prevalent in your culture. Various cults spring up from time to time (I'm talking about you, Scientology), and people sometimes convert to a completely different faith, or lose religious faith all together. Nonetheless, the general rule still holds true. People worship the God they were taught about by family and friends since childhood, the one that is part of their culture. That is how most people select the deity they will worship - without much conscious deliberation.

Most of these religions profess to speak on behalf of God, but the God they speak for is not the same one. Their deities have different likes, characteristics, rules for us, teachings, predictions, paths to happiness, religious practices and post mortem plans for us. In defense of their competing claims, there is no real proof of which is true, only belief and faith, reinforced by friends, relatives, associates, and the culture and society you happen to have been born into. They do however, have old traditions, writings, sayings, or scripture that are often cited as "proof", some of which we will consider in the next chapter.

What of the people who choose a deity or faith other than the one of their youth? How and why do people change churches or even go so far as to join a cult? A number of factors come into play. The strongest lure seems to me to be the sense of community and acceptance by the new church. We are social creatures and being accepted and welcomed by a group is inherently desirable and rewarding. Churches usually have various kinds of social events in addition to services, and often have smaller groups within the church that meet individual interests or needs. Often, people who leave a church were angered or put off by some event involving other church members, clergy, or policy. Sometimes they lacked strong ties to any church to begin with. Non religious people often turn to religion in times of personal crisis, making them a prime target for conversion. Converts often have a friend or associate who invites them to try their church or to study their faith. Leaving the newfound faith would likely result in the loss of the friendship, acceptance and emotional support they found in other members of that church. Whether it is a cult like Charles Mason's "family", "Moonies", or a mainstream church, the emotional and social needs of the convert play a key role in their conversion.

Churches sometimes offer the promise of healing when you or a loved one suffers from some physical malady. More recently, we have seen the rise of churches that promise followers financial prosperity. For the convert, the church (or cult) is filling a need, or at least offering hope that their need will be met. The greater a person's need, the greater their vulnerability and willingness to consider new doctrine and a new approach. After all, when you have hit rock bottom, you have nothing left to lose. A drowning man will grasp at anything to keep his head above water.

This much is certain. Believers do not select a deity to believe in by objectively reviewing a list of all deities, critically evaluating the evidence for each, and making a rational choice of which to believe in, worship, praise and follow. The decision is not rational or logical, and not based on evidence. It is an emotional decision. The arguments and evidence in support of that decision are gathered only after a decision has already been made for reasons that have little or nothing to do with evidence and rational arguments.

# CHAPTER 3

# Scripture

> Whether you are a believer—fundamentalist, evangelical,
> moderate, liberal—or a nonbeliever, the Bible is the
> most significant book in the history of our civilization.
> Coming to understand what it actually is, and is not,
> is one of the most important intellectual endeavors
> that anyone in our society can embark upon.
>
> — **Bart D. Ehrman**

**BEFORE DELVING TOO** deeply into scripture itself, I would ask the reader to consider a related question. If you believe in a deity, you likely believe this deity is omnipotent. Your God, if you believe in one, can do anything. He created the whole universe and everything in it, keeps it all humming along, and has power over life and death. He puts ideas in the heads of people if He so chooses, intervenes in everyday affairs, causes, permits or halts immensely powerful natural disasters and sometimes answers our prayers, even those that are silent, telepathic communications with Him. He reads minds, tracks everything you do and never forgets. God can cure cancer or any illness confronting any member of the human race. He can wipe out all of mankind or raise a man from the dead. He performs miracles that violate any law of nature whenever He chooses to do so. There are no limitations on his power, save apparently, one. He can't write a book, at least not all by Himself.

In order to communicate what He wants us to know about Him, our eternal destiny and what we should and should not do, He needs men to write a book on his behalf. Not only that, He needs men to edit it, selecting which parts were from Him and which weren't. Men are then needed to publish and distribute it, to translate those writings into our vernacular, and still other men to study it and explain to us what those writings really mean. Looking at the process objectively, it's hard to imagine how it would look any different if men came up with the whole thing themselves, without any divine help at all.

With that in mind, here's my question for the reader: if you were a deity who had a message you wanted all of mankind to receive and believe for as long as humans exist, would you convey your thoughts that same way? Could you think of a different way that would be un-ambiguous and not subject to all the confusion and misunderstandings that humans introduce into the message? If you were a deity, couldn't you just implant in human brains whatever you want them to know and believe? No printing, no translation, no interpretation, no copying errors, no errant or heretical writings in competition with yours, no ambiguity. If He could and didn't, why do you think He introduced all of those sources of confusion and error into what He actually wants us to know and believe? The method He chose to communicate guar-antees that some people will get the message wrong, a message that is crucial for salvation and one He supposedly wants us to have. We are left to wonder whether the message came from God and is important to understand correctly, or if God was unable or unwilling to concoct a better way to communicate His message. The easy way out of that question is to recite a platitude, like "God works in mysterious ways" or some other phrase that amounts to "I don't know". That is an abdication of your use of reason, one that avoids facing the truth, which is that it is unreasonable, irrational, and inconsistent with other beliefs you may hold about this deity. Put another way, it just doesn't make sense.

Different religions have different writings that they recognize as divinely inspired and sacred. Even within Christianity, different branches include different books in their bible, and use different translations. We also know there were many books and gospels that were well known to early Christians that never made it into the Bible. Whether your scripture is the Torah, Quran, the Bible, the Book of Mormon or something else, your scripture is the claim, not the proof of the claim. Your scripture asserts what happened, what your deity proclaims and teaches. It does not, in itself, prove the claim is true. Asserting that your scripture is true because your scripture says it is true and has divine authority is circular reasoning that isn't helpful to someone searching for answers. They all claim divine authority, and since they contradict each other, they can't all be true.

I am going to limit this discussion of scripture to the Bible, which is the most widely used and believed scripture in America. To some believers it is the literal word of God, while to others it is the inspired word of God. Some believe it is historically accurate, while to others, historical accuracy, with the possible exception of Jesus resurrection, is irrelevant and sometimes doubtful. Consequently, trying to determine exactly what Christians hold true about the Bible is like trying to nail jello to a tree. They are all over the map, despite the occasional protestation that differences in theology, interpretation, or teaching mean those who differ are not "real" Christians. That often makes it really hard to seriously discuss the Bible or Christianity with them, because you may feel like you are always shooting at a moving target. In fact, Christianity is a big tent that covers lots of differing beliefs.

One attribute most people ascribe to God is omniscience. He knows everything, not only about us, our conduct and our hearts' desires, but everything. He not only knows the laws of physics, he created them. Subatomic particles, biology, science, medicine, psychology, the past, the future, God knows everything. Yet consider the cosmology of the Bible.

The cosmology of the Bible was very primitive and nothing even close to what we now know about the universe. The earth was flat and rested on pillars. The land was surrounded on all sides by water. Below the surface of the earth was Sheol, the abode of the dead. Above the earth was the firmament, which was actually a dome that rested on mountains. It might help to imagine a cake plate on a pedestal with a domed cover over it. The sun, moon and stars were lights in the firmament. Above the firmament was more water. There were windows in the firmament that could be opened, allowing water to escape, thus causing it to rain on earth. Above that water, was heaven, the dwelling place of God. The way the cosmology of the Bible was written, it seems that the omniscient God who was its authoritative source, didn't know any more about science, physics, geology, or astronomy than the ignorant, scientifically illiterate people of ancient times who He used to write it.

This cosmology is described and alluded to in various places in the Bible. For example, you may recall that Jesus bodily ascended into heaven, rising up into the sky beyond the clouds. The obvious question in the 21st century, is where did He go then - turn left at the moon? Is he still in orbit? How did he get to heaven from there? With a round earth, he didn't really go up; he actually would have been going somewhat sideways. The answer lies here, in their understanding of cosmology. They believed heaven was an actual physical place, the world was flat, and if you floated straight up, you would get to heaven. So the story of what happened and how, was crafted around and assumed the primitive and erroneous beliefs they held. If the cosmology is wrong, the credibility of the whole story is called into question. Where did Jesus go, if it couldn't have happened as the Bible describes?

Religious texts include a lot of amazing, inexplicable events that directly contradict our experience of what is possible. Jesus walking on water, Moses parting a sea, people rising from the dead, physical maladies of every sort cured with a touch, a word, or a prayer. Then there's the talking snake, a talking donkey, the sun standing still for a day, a man living inside a large fish, a staff turned into a serpent and a woman turned into salt. Most of these stories would be dismissed out of hand without any serious consideration, unless 1) You were primitive, uneducated, superstitious, and lacked a way to reliably determine whether or not it was true, 2) You know the stories are impossible but have decided you want them to be true and profess them as such, choosing to ignore what you know, or 3) You were indoctrinated with the belief from childhood.

In the ancient world, people, especially common people, faced a world filled with dangers they could do little about. Women commonly died in childbirth, child mortality was high, and average life expectancy was much shorter than it is today. People lived under the constant threat of famine and plague. They lacked effective medicine, modern agricultural techniques, pesticides, or even a fundamental understanding of bacteria, viruses and how they were transmitted. Work days were hard and long, and taxes were onerous. Most people were illiterate and folklore took the place of education. With few books, no newspapers, TV, internet, radio or reporters, superstition reigned.

Causes and remedies were poorly understood and poorly evaluated for accuracy. In such a world, people believed many variations of what we know today, was nonsense.

We know that people struggle when dealing with conflicting evidence and beliefs. Research has shown us that people often rationalize away evidence that is contrary to what they have already accepted as true. It should come as no surprise then, that even today, people sometimes believe the impossible is true, despite evidence to the contrary that they are well aware of. I once had an English professor who said her religious beliefs were deeply held, and in direct conflict with other things she knew to be true. She recognized their incompatibility, and she just kept them separate. That's one approach. Compartmentalize conflicting beliefs, pronouncing both as true, without resolving the contradictions that make them mutually exclusive. However, it also insures you will never arrive at the truth, perhaps because you are afraid of what it might be.

That brings us to the effect of childhood indoctrination. If I told you that Mohammed ascended to heaven on a winged horse, you likely would dismiss that claim out of hand. You wouldn't waste a minute researching its truth, the historicity or translation of documents reporting the event, or looking for corroborating evidence. You might note the fact that winged horse fossils have never been discovered anywhere on earth. Of course a believer could explain the absence of fossil evidence by pointing out that if horses were winged, they could have flown to heaven to die. Still, you dismiss it as impossible, ridiculous. Yet Muslims believe it is true. The Temple Mount in Jerusalem is a holy site, and the place from which Mohammed supposedly ascended on that magical horse. A major difference between you and the Muslims of today who believe it, is they were indoctrinated with the story from childhood. When mom, dad, grandma, your religious leader, school teacher, friends and neighbors believe it and re-tell it as historically factual, well, it just doesn't seem so farfetched.

Carl Sagan was only partly right when he said that extraordinary claims require extraordinary evidence. It was not required in the ancient world among the primitive, uneducated and superstitious. Extraordinary evidence is also not required by those who have decided to follow what they want to be true. Neither is it required if one has been properly indoctrinated from an early age. In Catholic parlance, that indoctrination would be called "Christian Formation". Parents of the Protestant flavor often send kids to Sunday school, and in summer, to bible camp. There the children learn bible stories, memorize verses, and sing religious songs. Judaism has study through the synagogue, Hebrew school, and bar mitzvah tutors. They have their own religious holidays and ritualistic ways to celebrate them. These religions all operate on the same principle. They all make some provision for (select the verb of your choice) educating, forming, or indoctrinating children. It is the same process with the same result, no matter the verb you use to describe it. Extraordinary claims do require extraordinary evidence, but only for those who are able and willing to evaluate the evidence objectively.

As I write about indoctrination, the lyrics of a song from the musical South Pacific keep coming to mind. "You've got to be taught to hate and fear, you've got to be taught from year to year, it's got to be drummed in your dear little ear, you've got to be carefully taught. You've got to be taught before it's too late, before you are 6 or 7 or 8." Although the lyrics are about racial prejudice and not religious indoctrination, parents, churches, and societies have long recognized the importance of shaping children from a tender age to hold the beliefs they find desirable. Consider how many of us pledged allegiance to a flag because society deemed it important, before we even understood the meaning of what we were reciting, or were capable of evaluating any alternatives. We were similarly taught the "right" things to believe about religion and God with no understanding of any alternative beliefs, except that they were wrong and should be ignored and avoided.

Let's consider a few other aspects of the Bible that call into question whether it is a reliable source. Most of us have seen or perhaps experienced an exercise that involves telling a story from one person to another, sometimes called the telephone game. It usually starts with a story that is relayed to one participant. The first participant then tells the story to a second participant, who is hearing it for the first time. In turn, the second participant retells the story to a third participant, who is also hearing it for the first time. As the story is told from one person to the next, it inevitably changes. Details are forgotten or subtly changed, and information is misunderstood. The further it is passed down the line, the more it departs from the original. At the end of a line with only 5 or 6 participants, it often differs significantly from the original story, and sometimes bears little resemblance to it at all. What does that have to do with the bible?

Most scholars agree that the first written gospel was the gospel of Mark. Nobody knows exactly when it was written, and the best they can do is estimate. Most agree with the estimate that it was written around the year 70 CE, give or take a few years. That means the earliest gospel was written about 40 years after the events it describes occurred. That in turn, means the stories circulated by word of mouth for a full 40 years before anyone wrote them down. Nobody knows what was added, subtracted, or embellished upon in those four decades, but based on what we know about how faithfully stories are told and retold, there is very good reason to believe what was eventually written differs substantially from the original events.

We also know that once a gospel was finally written down, exactly what it said is anyone's guess. We don't know what it said, because we don't have the original, or even a copy of a copy of the original. The earliest fragment of a written gospel we have is a business card size fragment of the gospel of John that dates to 125 CE, though some date it later than that. John was the last gospel written, probably around 90 - 100 CE. That means the earliest written record we have is a tiny fragment of a copy of who knows how many copies, that was produced 30 years or so after the original was written, and 95 years after the events it describes occurred. The oldest reasonably complete copy of a written gospel we have dates to the year 200 CE, approximately 170 years after the events it reports happened.

Lest the reader think that written copies of stories are truer to the original than oral renditions, let's look at some of the evidence. The earliest written versions of the Gospel of Mark that we have, ended with Chapter 16 verse 8. Your bible doesn't. Everything in your bible after verse 8 was added later. Nobody knows who made the addition or why. In fact, there were two different endings - a longer ending, and a shorter one, sometimes called the "lost ending". Neither of those endings was included in the earliest manuscripts.

You may remember the story in John's gospel about the adulterous woman, in which Jesus was asked about stoning her, as Mosaic Law commanded. He said the man without sin should cast the first stone, which got her off the hook. There is good reason to be skeptical. The writing style and terminology is different from the rest of the gospel. That story isn't in any of the other gospels, and was not in the earliest versions we have of John's gospel. Someone added it in sometime later. We don't know who that someone was, if they heard the story from someone else and thought it would be a good addition, or if they made it up to make some theological point. In any case, that fabricated story is still included in what many people consider to be the inerrant Word of God. The reader would do well to ask why the story continues to be preached from pulpits, knowing that it was a later forgery. The answer may be reliance on authority or tradition, which also requires that fact, truth and scholarship be subordinated.

There were other texts in your bible that were not in the earliest versions we have, that were added in later by scribes who thought it would be a good idea to do so. For example, John 5:7 which describes the trinity was a later addition. Luke 24:51 which described the bodily ascension of Jesus was also a later addition to that gospel. The additions were made to clarify, to answer the claims of skeptics, or perhaps to settle a disputed theological question. Whatever the purpose, they were clearly forgeries, and forgeries that continue to be read and taught as the word of God in churches around the world.

We know that after escaping from Egypt, Moses led God's chosen people to the Promised Land through the desert. It took them 40 years to get there. That time period is sometimes interpreted to mean a generation, rather than a literal 40 trips around the sun. Do you know how far the Promised Land is from Egypt? You will probably be surprised if you check it out on Google. You can walk from Cairo to Jerusalem in less than 7 days. True, the roads are probably better now. Maybe Moses, like a lot of men, just wouldn't ask for directions. You can imagine thousands of maybes, but I challenge you honestly ask yourself if the story is credible. When answering that question, it may be useful to know that the Jews (the estimated number at that time is disputed but could have been as high as 2 million) supposedly wandered in a desert for 40 years and did not leave behind a single archaeological bit of evidence that they were there. Not a spear, a piece of pottery, a grave, evidence of an encampment, nothing. Another relevant fact is that Egyptian records and inscriptions do not corroborate the Exodus or the plagues that were supposedly called down on Egypt in association with that story. None of that proves the Exodus didn't happen; only that it is implausible and not supported by the evidence that is available outside of the Bible.

A brief review of the many gospels that didn't make it into the Bible provides abundant evidence that the people of that ancient, superstitious era were not above fabrication, even or perhaps especially, in matters of religion. They created stories for their own purpose, and used whatever pseudonyms supplied the necessary credibility. Stories and events were freely created or modified.

While we are on the topic of pseudonyms, here's a trick question. Who wrote the Pauline epistles? You might be inclined to say St. Paul. If so, you would only be partly correct. Some were written by Paul, some are of disputed authorship, but almost every scholar would agree that I Timothy, II Timothy and Titus were written by someone else who claimed to be Paul. These books are part of your bible. There's really no way to objectively determine whether or how this falsehood affected the claimed divine inspiration of the text, although it seems reasonable to question whether God would inspire a forgery and use it to convey His message. Still, they are considered scripture.

The letters of Paul are the earliest Christian writings we have. They pre-date the gospels and so give us some insight into what the earliest Christian beliefs were, and how they were different from the gospels that followed. We know Paul claimed to have met the risen Jesus in a vision. Interestingly, Paul makes no distinction between the way he and the apostles met the risen Jesus, only that he was the last to do so. The gospels tell us of a bodily raised Jesus who later bodily ascended to heaven. That might explain why we can't see or visit Him. Still, Paul's description raises a question of whether the whole resurrection was an ethereal, spiritual, resurrection rather than the bodily resurrection the gospels later described. In the ancient world, they thought of spirits as made of matter, unlike our modern conception of spirits. For Paul, flesh was not the same as body. Flesh was the part of us subject to and corrupted by sin. So, a resurrected body was composed of matter, but not flesh. That is something quite different from the resuscitated corpse many of us were taught to believe in.

Paul also makes no mention of the miracles Jesus performed. Nothing about raising Lazarus, healing the sick, walking on water, blind see, lame walk, virgin birth, loaves and fishes, none of that, even when it could have helped him make his point. Apologists have argued his letters were written to churches that would have already known the miracle stories, and were composed to address issues the churches were having. Accordingly, there was no reason for him to mention the miracles. That explanation leaves a glaring problem. The churches already knew about the crucifixion of Jesus, which Paul mentioned 13 times. They also knew about Jesus resurrection, which Paul mentioned 14 times in his letters. So the fact is, Paul did include things they would already know about in his letters. The absence of any miracle stories could well be because they never happened, and were later exaggerations added to persuade new converts. What we do see, is that as time went on, from Paul to the early gospels to the later gospels, the stories became more embellished, more magical, and more unlikely. That is remarkably similar to what we see in the telephone game.

We all know the nativity story that Mary and Joseph went to Bethlehem to be counted in a census, because Joseph was in the lineage of King David, so had to go there to be counted. We sing about it every Christmas, watch Christmas plays depicting the events, and can't drive very far without seeing a manger on someone's front lawn. The story is part of our culture. Sorry, but it's not true. When Romans conducted a census, it was for the purpose of taxation. They didn't know or care who your ancestor 30 generations previous was, or what town he was from. They didn't make you travel anywhere to be counted. In fact, they came to you. Requiring the kind of travel described in the Bible would have created chaos, not to mention lost tax revenue for Rome as workers went on their respective journeys to be counted. Of course, the story went a long way in explaining how the messiah could come from Nazareth, which was contrary to Jewish expectations for their messiah. They merely created a tale that resolved the objections they encountered, and surprise – Jesus of Nazareth *really* came from Bethlehem. When describing the Nativity, both Matthew and Luke describe Jesus' lineage. Most of us skip over the long lists of who begot who. Those who are sticklers for detail have noticed that the two genealogies are radically different. Matthew has 27 generations from David to Joseph, while Luke has 42. They don't even agree on who Joseph's father was.

I have a friend who dislikes musicals, because they are not, in his view, realistic. In the real world, people don't fall in love, then suddenly break out in song, accompanied by an orchestra. True enough. Most life events don't happen in an area as small as a theatrical stage either. If you have ever been inside a real structure fire, as I have, it is nothing like the ones usually portrayed on TV shows, because if they portrayed it realistically, you wouldn't be able to see much on your screen except dark smoke. You may have seen a show in which someone was shot with a handgun and propelled backward with great force, through a glass door or window. In reality, that defies the laws of physics and never happens. Every action has an equal and opposite reaction. If it had enough force to knock the bad guy in the air and off his feet, it would have the same effect on the good guy who shot the gun. Theatrical productions require that you suspend your disbelief and stop thinking critically, in order to enjoy the show. They take liberties with facts and reality to make a better story. We might apply that same explanation to the Bible, but it isn't theatre according to most believers. It is the word of God, historical and factual, though the next story could lead you to doubt that assertion.

The tale I like to call "The Jerusalem Zombies", is a real New Testament story, and though believers refer to the event using other terms, that's exactly what it is. According to Matthew 27:52-53, when Jesus died, many tombs of dead saints were opened and they were raised from the dead. Later, after Jesus' resurrection, they went into Jerusalem and appeared to many people. There's no word on why they waited 2 days to go into town; maybe zombies need to stretch a while before taking walks. If this actually occurred, it would have been among the most newsworthy, historic, and widely shared events in history. If many people rose from the dead, came to town and were seen by many others, it's not the kind of event people would keep secret. Yet it is not recorded in a single Jewish historical record, or a single Roman historical record. It is not even in another gospel, only Matthew's. There are no references to this event in any of the Christian epistles, or in any of the many gospels that didn't make it into the Bible. No inscriptions, no documents referring to the event, nothing. One of the most incredible events to occur in the history of mankind, and nobody, except the author of Matthew, thought to make mention of it. For those reasons, even most Christian scholars doubt it actually occurred.

In Ecclesiastes, the Bible teaches us that what has been done before will be done again; there is nothing new under the sun. Perhaps, except that organ transplants, antibiotics, space travel and computers are pretty new. Well, that and nuclear weapons, pizza, the internal combustion engine, television, microwave ovens and socialized medicine. Then there's Social Security, welfare, the 40 hour work week and air travel. OK, the scientific method, accepting homosexuals and minorities as worthwhile human beings, accepting women as equals to men and abolishing slavery. But the Bible tells us there is nothing new.

Ken Ham is a Christian who is singularly committed to proving that the creation story, the story of the great flood, and the entire book of Genesis is literally true. I think he has it right when he says that if those stories aren't historically accurate, it calls into question what else in the Bible is merely a myth, metaphor or legend. For that reason, he sees a lot at stake in proving the events of Genesis were factual. He certainly has his work cut out for him. For starters, Genesis includes two different and conflicting accounts of creation. The amount of water required for the great flood is roughly 3 times the amount of water on and within earth and its atmosphere. Where did all of that water come from, and where did it go after the flood? Note that question is much less problematic if you accept the ancient cosmology that we know is false, whereby the windows in the firmament could open and dump it out. The ark described isn't big enough to accommodate all the animals it supposedly carried, let alone food and water for all of them. How did animals that only live in remote places like Australia or the Arctic, make it to the Middle East to get on the ark? What did predatory animals eat when they were on and after they got off got off the ark? Their prey was wiped out in the flood, and eating any of the other animals that were on the ark would have resulted in the extinction of the species they ate. Water droplets didn't refract light (the mechanism by which light produces rainbows) until after the flood. It just doesn't add up, if you allow yourself to think about it. Some would encourage you not to think about it, just believe. Pay no attention to things that don't add up, don't use your reason, ignore the claims you know are not factual, turn your brain off, it will make you pleasing to God, or at least to them.

When confronted with the fact that these Bible stories are

impossible as described, apologists sometimes reply that "God made it happen" though they don't know how, and tell us that "with God, all things are possible". That is shorthand for "I know it is impossible as far as we know and can prove, but I want it to be true, and it is what I have decided to believe". It is equally true that with imagination, all things are possible.

Perhaps even more glaring are the two promises Jesus supposedly made, that are obviously false. The first is that whatever followers ask for in prayer in His name will be granted. It's in several different places, worded slightly differently, but there's no doubt what the promise was. That's why Christians pray in Jesus name all the time. Apologists have asserted that what Jesus said wasn't really what he meant, of necessity. It isn't true, hasn't happened, and they know it. Either Jesus lied, he didn't really make the promise that the gospels say he made, or he must have meant something other than what it says. Since the first two options are out of the question for them, they have to find a way to interpret away the plain language of the assurance Jesus gave to His followers.

The second unfulfilled promise is that He would return before this generation, the one He was speaking to, passed away. Again, phrased slightly differently in different places, but the declaration is clear. Early Christians certainly believed Jesus return was imminent. They were wrong. Again, apologists struggle to reinterpret what he meant, because what He clearly said He would do never happened. They sometimes quote 2 Peter as saying that for God a day is like a thousand years. That does nothing to invalidate the plain language of the promise. It also ignores that 2 Peter is a forgery, a fact agreed to by most biblical scholars. Everyone has their own internal B.S. detector. Some of us make a conscious decision to turn ours off and ignore the evidence. Still others, who find themselves unable to ignore it, rationalize and interpret the evidence away. For me, the weight of the evidence eventually became too great to ignore, deny, rationalize or interpret away, and I had to face it along with its implications.

Objectivity and fairness require that I inform the reader that there is only one Gospel of the Flying Spaghetti Monster. We know when it was written, by whom, and there are no translation difficulties between the original and modern day English. It was not handed down by word of mouth for decades before being written. No suspicious deletions or additions have been made. Not a single scholar has called into question any aspect of its authenticity. I will leave it to the reader to judge for themselves which of the gospels is more plausible. As our evangelical brothers have proclaimed on the question of teaching "creation science" in schools, students should be provided with all of the conflicting views, information and evidence, and then be allowed to make their own decision about what to believe.

# CHAPTER 4

# Interpretation of Scripture

Never trust the translation or interpretation of
something without first trusting its interpreter.

— **Suzy Kassem**

**AT THIS POINT** we are left with a book that has been deemed to be holy, filled with stories and edicts, many of which are doubtful, at least some of which we know were altered and some of which we are reasonably certain are not factual, that many people believe is the literal or inspired word of God. How do we interpret the meaning and significance of the words and use them to guide the faithful who believe it? Not surprisingly, there are some different views on that question. We do know that the Bible discusses so many topics and circumstances, that one can find a verse or verses that can be interpreted to support almost anything you want. Look no further than the days of slavery in America, when slave owners and abolitionists both used the Bible to support their position. As Shakespeare wrote, the devil can cite scripture for his purpose.

One approach to interpreting scripture is the Ken Ham or the fundamentalist school of interpretation. Using that approach, the Bible is the literal and inerrant word of God, period. Everything in it literally happened, is literally and historically factual, and it should be interpreted literally. This approach is pretty straightforward, and also pretty difficult to defend. Think back to the cosmology of the Bible. Sorry, but the world is not flat, there is no firmament, and heaven is not a place above it. We've been in space far above the clouds, and there's no heaven there. Both creation stories in Genesis cannot be literally true. The world is not 6,000 years old. There are different accounts of the same event throughout the Bible that can't be simultaneously true. At least one of the accounts, or possibly both of them, is false.

The notion that the Bible should be read literally, without interpretation, is an impossible way to understand language. For example, consider Matthew 23:9, which says you should call no man your father on earth, for one is your father who is in heaven. You could read it literally to mean your mother conceived you without the participation of your biological father. It could be taken literally to restrict the terms you can use to refer to your biological male parent. I had one person apply the verse to the Catholic practice of addressing their priests with the title "Father", as proof that they are not a Bible believing faith. It probably meant that people should not place revered religious leaders or their teachings over God. But any way you slice it, the words must be interpreted to understand what the message was, and there may be several different "literal" interpretations.

This school of "literal" interpretation runs headlong into conflicts with observable, empirical, facts from fields such as geology, archaeology, anthropology, biology, psychology, and history. For example, the Old Testament clearly indicates homosexuality is an abomination. Today, we have evidence that homosexuality is not a choice, sinful or otherwise. There is evidence of neurological differences between heterosexuals and homosexuals, genetic and chromosomal differences, a significant fraternal birth order effect in male homosexuals, and evidence of gestational hormonal influences in female homosexuals. Homosexuality has been observed in many non-human species as well. That raises the question of whether it is also a sinful abomination when non-human species engage in homosexual acts. When discussing the freedom with which someone chose to be homosexual, a point is often made by asking someone when they chose to be heterosexual. They didn't. It's just how they are. Homosexuality is likely just a normal variation in how people are made. That modern understanding is hard to square with God's revelation on the matter, as proclaimed by illiterate Bronze Age goat herders who didn't know where the sun went at night.

Another popular approach to interpreting the Bible is personal revelation. The notion is that the reader is led by the Holy Spirit to correctly understand the message and appropriate interpretation. This is often done in conjunction with bible study groups. Of course, many people can claim such divine inspiration, all the while reaching different interpretations. That means either some or all of them are making the claim of divine inspiration falsely, or the Holy Spirit is deliberately trying to confound believers, which would seem counter to His purpose. Assuming some of the claims of spirit filled insight are false, the rest of us are left without an objective way to determine which of their interpretations, if any, are actually inspired and correct. Most often, people believe the interpretation of the religious tradition their parents believed, which is the religious tradition their parents before them believed, which nobody can conclusively prove to be the correct tradition. It's merely what "we" believe.

Another approach to interpreting the Bible is reliance on authority. Clergy have been trained and given the authority to teach on behalf of their church. The church has been given the authority by God (Matthew 16: 18-19). When the correct interpretation of a passage is not clear, authority is the tie breaker that enables us to safely determine what is true. The pope, in certain circumstances and matters involving faith and morals, is infallible and cannot be wrong, at least according to Catholic doctrine. The early church had many gospels floating around, some quite popular, that were later determined to be non-canonical, as well as clergy who had different and conflicting theological views. They often relied on authority to proclaim what was heresy and what was not. I find the most compelling argument against this reliance on authority in a single word; "transubstantiation".

You may recall the last supper in which Jesus broke bread, said "this is my body", gave it to His disciples, told them eat it, and to do that in memory of him. Transubstantiation is a word created to explain or describe Catholic doctrine about this practice. In brief, when a man who has been duly authorized performs a specified ritual and incantation, the wafers he performs it on become the actual body of a Jew who was killed 2,000 years ago. It may look like a wafer and taste like a wafer, chemical tests you did on it would verify that it is indistinguishable from a wafer, but it isn't. It only appears to be a wafer. How could it give every appearance of being one thing but actually be something else? Transubstantiation. Don't believe your own eyes, your senses, your reason, the heretics who disagree, or even chemistry. Believe only the authority who proclaimed this doctrine. That may sound silly if you are a Baptist, Muslim or Jew, but if it was part of your childhood indoctrination, it makes perfect sense. There is even a word to describe the phenomena. This is an example of the sort of interpretation you get by relying on authority to the exclusion of your own use of evidence and reason.

Another similar pronouncement is the Trinity. Most ancient religions believed in a variety of gods who reigned over different areas of human concern. They were often interchangeable, and people of one culture worshipped the deities of another as a matter of social courtesy when visiting each other. Judaism and Zoroastrianism were unique in the ancient world, in that they were monotheistic. There was only one deity who oversaw everything, and the worship of any other deity was prohibited. Along comes Christianity, rooted in Judaism, which seems to contradict a basic tenet of that faith, monotheism. Christianity now has the God of the Jews (the father), but also a son (Jesus) who is divine, and a third divinity, the Holy Spirit. The contradiction was addressed with the invention of the trinity. Ok, sure there are now three Gods, but they are actually only one God. They are distinct, but one and the same. How could that be? It's a mystery. He'll let us know after we die. In the meantime, just believe it. Have faith. The Church has pronounced it is true. To allay any doubts, it was even added into the bible (1 John 5:7) even though we know it was not in the earliest Greek manuscripts. The impossible and inconceivable is true, and we have even invented a word for it: Trinity.

Disagreement with the proclamations of religious authority aside, an obvious problem with relying on authority is determining who the appropriate authority is, how that determination should be made, and who is to make it. Both Christianity and Islam have struggled with that problem for centuries, and have yet to achieve a resolution within either faith. Different authorities with different views have been accepted by different sects within both religions. Without any agreed upon method to identify the authority, the bystander is left to guess which "authority" is the real one with the correct answers, who should be trusted and followed.

A fourth approach to scriptural interpretation is reliance on scholarship. Most of the words spoken in the Bible were originally spoken in Hebrew or Aramaic. When first written down, the New Testament was written in Greek. It was subsequently translated into Latin, and then

English. Things can get lost in translation, because different languages don't always have equivalent words with exactly the same meaning. Often, a word can have several meanings depending on the context in which it is used. Consider also, that language changes over time. I once asked my mother in law, who immigrated to the US from Poland after WWII, to translate a letter that was written in Polish for a friend of mine. My mother in law pointed out to me that there was a difference between the Polish that she spoke in the 1940's and the Polish spoken by native Poles 60 years later. An English equivalent might be that in 1950, saying a person was gay meant they were carefree and cheerful. The term had nothing to do with their sexual orientation, as it does today. Languages changed in similar ways in antiquity. There are scholars who have studied these ancient languages, and use that knowledge to help us understand how to interpret the writings. One example of how scholarship leads to such understanding is in the writings of St. Paul. When Paul said we aren't saved by works, he was referring to circumcision and Jewish dietary laws, not to good deeds, contrary to the common evangelical interpretation of "works".

Scholars compare and date texts and fragments, including those from non biblical sources. They study the ancient history, geography and cultures. They also obtain, study and evaluate archaeological evidence. In sum, they study all of the available information and draw conclusions based on that information. My view is that this approach is the one most likely to lead us to the right conclusions about what really happened, what was really said, and what it meant. I say that with two caveats.

The first caveat is that most biblical scholars pursued those studies because they were already convinced of the truth of Christianity and committed to it. Most biblical scholars were trained by other scholars who also shared that faith. Accordingly, most such scholars are predisposed to look at the evidence through the lens of what they have already declared is true. They are after all only human, and human beings share some well known predispositions. We know from the psychological theory of cognitive dissonance, that when faced with evidence that contradicts beliefs we already hold, our natural tendency is to try to dismiss the evidence. On the other hand, when evidence confirms beliefs we already hold, we tend to accept it without as much critical evaluation.

The second caveat is that the evidence is often mixed; there may be evidence that both confirms and refutes a particular interpretation or assertion, especially when we are dealing with ancient history. Scholars sometimes disagree, mainly on the issue of which piece of evidence is most important or compelling, and most consistent with other things we are pretty certain of. In the end, we may have arguments, but not definitive answers. We don't really know, and certainty, unless more information becomes available, is sometimes unattainable.

Although it is not really scholarly, one example of how the learned can get carried away is in "harmonizing" the gospels. That is, interpreting them so that seemingly contradictory passages are no longer in conflict and both can be true. Here is how it works. You start with the assumption that there are no contradictions in the Bible, which is the inerrant, or at least inspired, word of God. Only those who don't understand the Bible think there are contradictions, and they are wrong in that belief. We then consider passages in different books that "seem" to be contradictory. For example, John's gospel says Mary Magdalene went to the tomb of Jesus, and the other gospels mention several women who went with her. So did Mary go alone, as John's gospel claims, or as part of a group as the others report? I know.....there were two trips. That's it...that's the ticket. Mary Magdalene went alone as described in John, and then went back, got the others, and made a second trip, which is the one described in the other gospels. How do I know that is what happened, you might ask. I don't. I pulled it out of thin air. I imagined it. But it resolves the apparent contradiction, so it must be what happened, because as we know, there are no contradictions.

Let's try another harmonization. John's gospel says the walk to the tomb of Jesus occurred when it was still dark, and the other gospels say it was early in the morning or just after dawn. That is only a contradiction to people who haven't studied the Bible and lack the proper understanding. "How is that not a contradiction?", you might ask. One story, John's, describes the time of day / lack of sunlight when the walk began, and the others describe when it ended and they arrived at the tomb. How do you know that? Again, you don't. But it "harmonizes" the accounts, eliminating the "apparent" contradiction, so it must be the correct understanding. See how that works? The only requirements necessary to harmonize gospels are a good imagination, the mere possibility it could have occurred the way you imagined, and a willingness to assert it as fact.

Another view that some hold, is that the Bible is not the inspired word of God all the time. There are contradictions, but they don't matter, as they don't involve core theological doctrines. Eyewitness accounts of any incident vary, so it's not surprising that the gospels sometimes differ. That sounds reasonable. Of course, this view brings the problem Ken Ham is afraid of into play. That is, if some parts of the Bible are wrong, contradictory, or simply metaphors, what else is wrong, what else didn't happen or wasn't spoken the way it says? How do you know any of it is true if you admit some of it isn't? Would God really inspire someone to report events incorrectly? Did He only inspire some parts but not others, and how would you know which parts those are? Ham is right, in that once you pull that thread, the whole garment starts to unravel.

Some scholars have suggested that at least some of the differences between the gospels are rooted in the differing theologies subscribed to by the authors, rather than differing perspectives and recollections of witnesses to actual events. I would argue that is all the more reason to doubt the gospels. The starting point should be what is true, what was said and what happened, and the theology should flow from that. Instead, they started with a theological belief, and crafted the story of the actual events around it.

There is only one gospel whose interpretation has never been contested by any scholar, that has no internal contradictions, and requires no harmonizing. That is the Gospel of the Flying Spaghetti Monster. Some have questioned whether all of the contents are factual. The author himself has clearly explained that those objectively questionable items were put in deliberately, to test your faith.

# CHAPTER 5

# Apologetics

We can't avoid reasoning; we can only avoid doing it well."
— Peter Kreeft

**APOLOGETICS, FROM THE** Greek term for speaking in defense of oneself, is a practice that defends religious doctrine through argumentation and discourse. Christians have been working on their apologetics for some 2,000 years. After two millennia of creating "evidence" and refining arguments, they have an answer for every doubt you may have about their beliefs. Any questions, doubts or criticism you may express about Christian teachings are neither new nor original, and neither are their answers. Those answers may not be satisfactory, may contradict historical evidence or may be incredulous, but they have an answer, often several different answers. For people who want it to be true, the apologist doesn't need an answer that he can prove is true. He only needs one that could be possible. That burden of proof is not burdensome at all. Any hypothesis that is unsupported by any evidence, but which can't be positively disproven, will suffice.

The apologist may invite you to their church for a visit. They are trying to win converts, souls for their God, an eternal reward for you, and perhaps give you some earthly respite from your troubles, whatever they may be. What tactics serving such noble purpose could be wrong? They may hand you a tract, which is a small booklet with a brief, easy to read Christian message, usually in a comic strip type of format. I once saw a tract depicting a curvy woman as bait on a fish hook, luring in males who she could catch for Jesus. That tactic works, and many men, including myself, have been persuaded to visit an evangelical church by a female love interest. The church members view visitors as potential converts, and will be friendly and try to make you feel comfortable. We are social animals after all, and a whole community of friends is inherently appealing.

You may also be invited to a bible study. If you really want to understand the Bible, this is the worst way to do so. Why? You are with a group of friends or would be friends, good people to all appearances, who know more about it than you do, have often been trained in converting the skeptic, and who you don't want to alienate by disagreeing. Just as if you were discussing the emperor's clothes, you can expect they will be nodding in agreement with each other, perhaps chiming in with their own insights into how beautiful and elegant the emperor's clothes (or the biblical interpretations) are. You are outnumbered, and won't hear any dissenting opinions, at least none that pose a serious challenge to their faith. Any challenges you hear will be a straw man argument – one they phrase and set up in such a way that they easily knock it down and make it look foolish. They have you right where they want you. Social psychologists have studied the impact of subtle group pressures and repeatedly verified the human reluctance to stand apart from the group. It is a well known and well researched phenomena.

The best advice I could give anyone is, when they tell you to just open your heart and let Jesus in, because he's there knocking at the door, "Run". What they mean is, stop thinking critically, stop evaluating, stop questioning, and believe what makes you feel good, just as we do. Truth, facts and history should all take a backseat to what is emotionally pleasant. Simply ignore your doubts and take the leap. We will all be there with you. Once you have made a decision and commitment to their beliefs, the psychological disposition we all share will steer you to dismiss conflicting information. That is the purpose served by rituals such as baptism and altar calls. That which you have publicly committed to, you will defend rather than continue to evaluate objectively or critically. After millennia of work, apologists have developed many defenses, tactics and arguments that you can learn.

One apologist tactic you may hear early on is an effort to lower the bar with respect to proof and evidence. Success in this effort allows them to submit evidence that is plausible or merely possible, and for you to accept that as sufficient. Their argument is that the "proof" we accept in everyday life is rarely absolute certainty or beyond any doubt. Instead, we often rely on evidence that may be supportive of a position, even if it is not conclusive. What is likely or probable is sufficient evidence to make a choice. We often rely on what others have told us, without requiring proof. The apologist may even admit that they can't prove the existence of God with absolute certainty. Just as in many other aspects of our lives, we should go with what seems most plausible, or most likely, even if we don't know for sure. It all sounds quite reasonable.

The obvious reason for that strategy is that it makes their job of persuading you much easier. Their approach itself is weak and should be rejected. Yes, a friend who is a football fan may tell me the outcome of a game I missed, and I accept their report without requiring further proof, such as a videotape of the game. However, I know he is a fan, likely watched the game, and he has no reason to lie to me about it. I also know the team exists and that they actually played a game on the date in question. Even if I do, I am not required to take his word for it. There are authoritative sources I can reference to verify his report with absolute certainty, if I so choose. Had my friend told me that a football game was played invisibly, somewhere outside of space and time, he knows the outcome because it was reported in some ancient scroll, and the final score was 350 to nothing, I would have some pretty serious doubts. In addition, the things I accept as true with minimal evidence, such as my friend's report on the outcome of a game, are inconsequential. They don't cost me, for example,10% of my income. They don't change my behavior, political views, child rearing practices or relationships. They certainly don't become a cornerstone on which I build the rest of my beliefs about the world and my life.

A popular apologist argument is that there is more evidence to support the resurrection of Jesus than there is for the Trojan War, yet nobody doubts the Trojan War. Perhaps so, as evidence of ancient historical events goes, considering how much time elapsed between the event and the documents reporting it, and the number of documents that reference the event. Don't stop there. Consider also, the plausibility of the events. We know that there were lots of wars throughout the history of the ancient world, so one more is certainly within the realm of possibility, perhaps even probable. In contrast, we also know that nobody alive has ever witnessed a corpse resurrected from the dead. Such an event is beyond our experience and is impossible based on everything we know from science. We also know that superstitious people in the ancient world made many claims of miraculous, magical events, including many such claims by pagans and other faiths that Christians dismiss as not being credible. What the apologist argument overlooks, and I believe deliberately so, is that the two events (a war and a bodily resurrection) are not equally plausible. Remember that apologists are defending what they already believe and trying to persuade others, not seeking the truth by objectively evaluating the evidence. That part is up to you.

By way of analogy, consider a parent of twins who finds damage to the bumper of his car. One twin says his brother was driving in a parking lot and bumped into a light pole. The other twin says he was parked in a parking lot when an angel from heaven flew down, struck the car with a sledge hammer, and warned him against becoming too attached to material objects, before ascending back into heaven. You have the same amount of evidence to support either claim; a damaged car, and the testimony of one person as to what happened. The difference lies in their plausibility. One account clearly describes a commonly observed event, and the other an event none of us have ever seen or had reliably reported to us. Even without that distinction, most people would require a great deal more evidence to accept the implausible account, and rightfully so. An explanation that contradicts things we already know to be true about the world and how things occur in it *should* be met with skepticism, and accepted only with abundant and compelling evidence. Most parents already know and apply this principle when dealing with their children, if not when dealing with their clergy.

I have had many online discussions with theists. An oft repeated statement goes something like this: "I am sorry for whatever it was that happened in your life that was so hurtful or painful that it caused you to (hate, reject or be angry with) God". It might include some seemingly kind wish or promise, like "God still loves you", "He will be there for you when you are ready", "I will pray for you", etc. This tactic, and it is a tactic, assumes there is something wrong with you, some traumatic experience warped you, and that is the reason you hate God. There must be some psychological pathology and anger underlying your lack of faith.

OK, look. I could similarly apologize for whatever happened in their life that caused them to adopt an imaginary friend. That knife cuts both ways. But don't pass over their erroneous assumption; that we disagree with them because of an event that produced hatred or anger with God. I don't hate God, any more that I hate the tooth fairy. I don't believe there is one. Nobody hates or is angry with a being that they don't believe exists. Most people are pretty much emotionally neutral about the Loch Ness Monster. They simply don't think there is one. The apologist's error is deliberate and purposeful, and puts the nonbeliever on the defensive. When they get lucky, it gets the skeptic wondering if there really is something wrong with them. After all, painful emotional experiences are a universal part of life, and perhaps they are right in asserting that mine are the reason for my disbelief. Rest assured, if you accept their assumption that there is something wrong with you, they will have the "cure" for it.

Some have claimed that if there were no God, we would need to invent one to have an orderly society with morality, compassion, and the like. As Dostoyevsky once wrote, "without God, all things are permitted". I agree with Dostoyevsky. Without a deity proclaiming right or wrong, everything is permitted and everything is on the table, at least until *we* prohibit it.

With that in mind, the apologist might argue that without God, there is no objective basis for morality. What you may call morality is just a personal preference. Some believe that atheists can have no sense of morality and are inherently untrustworthy, not sharing religious values, such as honesty, compassion, love, the golden rule, etc. Some jurisdictions within the United States, for that reason, have passed laws banning atheists from holding public office.

I am not concerned about whether morality lacks an objective basis without a deity who imposes it on us. So what? As long as the rules for our behavior work, they have served their purpose. There is no need for God to justify the wisdom of the rules we agree to live by. As long as they provide the social cohesion that is their primary purpose, it doesn't matter whether they were handed to Moses on stone tablets, given to us through a prophet, or if the rules were passed by elected legislators who thought it was a good way for us to live together. Those who cling to the need for objective morality fail to recognize that the morality they subscribe to also lacks objectivity. The existence of the deity they believe in and that deity's edicts have not been objectively proven. That which they have chosen to believe as a matter of faith is itself not objective by definition.

Creationists in particular, like to challenge different fields of science, knowing full well most of us aren't experts in all of these fields. They often do this by pointing to an anomaly in a field of study which is factually true. The uninitiated have no way of recognizing the fact that they are pointing to a case that is an exception to the rule, rather than proof the rule is wrong. This is sometimes referred to as the "cherry picking fallacy", in which you point to a single piece of evidence that seems to confirm your position, while ignoring the greater body of evidence that refutes it. Recognizing that is occurring would require you develop a thorough understanding of some esoteric discipline that you may know very little about. You would have to understand the field of study in question to understand why the factoid they point to is insignificant and contrary to the body of knowledge in the field. It's a bit like someone pointing to an individual who smoked their whole life and lived to be 100, as proof that smoking does not pose a health risk. To understand what is wrong with that analysis, you would have to understand a lot about data analysis, sample size, measures of central tendency, statistical significance, contradictory evidence and research methods. For most of us who don't already know those things, delving deeply into a new discipline simply won't happen. Once the factoid is put out there, often by a believer with an advanced degree struggling to reconcile their faith with scientific fact, it spreads. People who also don't fully understand the significance of the factoid add it to their repertoire of defenses, preach it from their pulpits, teach it in bible schools, and incorporate it into various types of publications.

One such example from the creationist book of tricks is to prove that radiometric dating is not reliable (and thus the earth could actually be only 6,000 years old), by pointing out the case of rock from a lava flow in Hawaii of a known age that was tested. The errant test results showed it was far older than it really was. That is true, as far as it goes. Consequently, the claim is quoted, cited and repeated over and over again in creationist publications to debunk radiometric dating and "prove" it is unreliable. The case they are citing is well known in the scientific community and recognized as an anomaly that does not invalidate radiometric dating, which is still regarded as highly reliable by the experts in the field. Here's what happened. The lava flow in question was unusual, in that it contained xenoliths that are foreign to the lava, carried from deep within the earth, but not completely melted by the lava. Further, because of excess bubbles trapped inside, xenoliths can't be accurately dated by the method (Potassium - Argon) that was used in this example. So in one unusual case, there was a contaminated sample, tested with the wrong dating method, which produced an inaccurate result. It's a little like doing a pregnancy test on a stool sample, and concluding pregnancy tests are invalid. Of course, if you have no expertise in radiometric dating and the apologist sounds like they do, you might be inclined to accept their critique. Like the memes that we all see on social media, how many does the average person have the time or inclination to fact check?

Another creationist argument is to point to Piltdown man, a dead horse that they have been beating for over half a century. Piltdown man was a fraudulent 1912 "discovery" presented as a missing evolutionary link. It was actually the skull of a human with a small brain, and the jaw and teeth of an orangutan. It wasn't uncovered as a fraud until 1953. Creationists like to make great hay out of the fact that one of the many thousands of pieces of fossil evidence supporting evolution was fabricated and accepted by science as factual. To them, a single instance of fraud, discovered and exposed by the same scientists who are experts in evolution, is sufficient to dismiss the entire body of scientific evidence. Not that they are familiar with the entire body of evidence; they just need one factoid to justify their claim that it is *all* wrong, or at least doubtful.

Creationists will sometimes say they believe in micro evolution, but not macro evolution. Again, you need to understand the evidence and the science. Macro evolution is the point at which an animal has evolved enough to be scientifically categorized as a new species. Micro evolution is simply all of the evolution that occurred before that point. It is exactly the same process, the same chain of events, just a change of terminology when it reaches a specific degree of change. To use an analogy, it's like claiming you believe heating water over a fire makes the water hot, but you don't believe it makes water boil, the point when it reaches 212 degrees. Micro evolution has been observed since the time of Darwin and is factually undeniable. What they are denying is the continuation of that evolution that they haven't witnessed, which takes much longer to occur and can't be witnessed in a single person's lifetime, even though it is evident in the fossil record. It is not a different kind or type of evolution, as they imply, but a matter of degree in exactly the same process.

How many factoids like these does the average person have the time and energy to study? We can't all develop an in depth understanding of every complex field. Your ignorance works in the favor of believers, who don't usually understand the field of study any better than you do – they just memorized useful tidbits in their study of apologetics. The safest approach is to be very skeptical of anything the religious say when using science to validate their religious claims, or to discredit scientific evidence in conflict with them. We know the tactic and how it is used, if not all the complexities of that particular field of study. We have examples that demonstrate when a scientist uses science to defend his religious beliefs, he's likely either misrepresenting the totality of the scientific evidence or is not a very good scientist and operating on the fringes (or outside) of his field.

"How do you explain the empty tomb?" is a question Christian apologists like to ask and expect you won't be able to answer. The inability to provide a satisfactory alternative explanation to theirs will lead to the conclusion that Jesus must have been raised from the dead, which is proof that he was the messiah and validates all the other Christian beliefs, like a row of falling dominoes. There is a fundamental flaw with is type of argument; it assumes an explanation that defies every law of nature and has never been reliably witnessed must be true, if you can't otherwise explain it. Suppose for example, I heard a noise coming from inside my closet last night, and attributed it to the boogeyman. Using their approach, if you can't explain what caused the noise, then by default, my explanation that it was the boogeyman must be correct. Therein lies the flaw. Any explanation for an event must stand on its own merits and the evidence for it. When we don't have a credible explanation, the default answer is "we don't know"; not an alternative explanation that is itself without merit or solid evidence.

The empty tomb question itself assumes that the biblical story of Jesus being crucified and buried in a tomb that Joseph of Arimathea provided is factual. The reasons to question that are abundant. First, we know that other deities in the ancient world supposedly died and resurrected. Jesus resurrection from the dead is only one of many such tales. The Christian must believe that while there are many such tales, the one he believes in is the only one that actually happened, and all the others are myths. Second, consider Christian scripture about the event. In the earliest gospel, Mark, Jesus was tried before the Sanhedrin, and they *all* condemned him. That means every single member, without exception. Joseph of Arimathea was a member of the Sanhedrin. The inescapable conclusion from Mark's gospel, is that Joseph of Arimathea was one of those who condemned Jesus. One might wonder why a member of the Sanhedrin condemned Jesus to death, yet was also a follower (Matt 27:57) and gave him a tomb. That was resolved by the time Luke's gospel was written, decades later, when Joseph became a dissenting voice in the Sanhedrin. Mark's and Luke's accounts cannot both be true. The most plausible explanation for the discrepancy is that Luke's account was written later and in a way that addressed the objections of doubters.

Where exactly was Arimathea? Good question. Nobody knows. Two ruined cities have been suggested as possible sites, but there is no conclusive proof for either. We know where Bethlehem, Nazareth, and Jerusalem were, but not Arimathea, or even if there really was a city of that name. The reader may consider that the word itself has sometimes been translated as "a good man" and "a city in Judea". All of the uncertainty, contradictions and ambiguities only add to the likelihood that the whole story, which defies everything we know about biology and science, and describes events that have never verifiably occurred in all of recorded history, is mythical.

We do know what Romans usually did. Crucifixion was a fate reserved for those who posed a threat to Roman rule; revolting slaves and insurgents; not robbers, thieves, or those holding unorthodox religious views. It was supposed to be as horrible and cruel as possible. On a cross, you had to push up with your legs to breathe. That is why breaking their legs would hasten their death. Scourging was done beforehand so the wounded back rubbed against the wood and caused excruciating pain every time they inhaled or exhaled. There would be no respite from the pain as long as the condemned continued to breathe. The inscription on a cross was not mocking, but a warning so everyone would know the fate awaiting anyone who undertook similar actions. After death, the body was typically left hanging to rot and be consumed by birds, dogs and other scavengers, adding to the horror of their fate. If removed, which may have happened to avoid inflaming religious sensitivities, they may have been entombed, may have been thrown on the dump outside the city that was always smoldering, or buried in an unmarked grave. Any of those possibilities are more plausible than the biblical story.

Many atheists believe Jesus never really existed at all and was just a mythical figure, supported by scholars such as Richard Carrier. If one accepts their view, the question of the empty tomb is even easier to explain. Of course, if Jesus was a historical person around whom many incredible myths and legends later rose, there really is no practical distinction, and the difference is purely academic. We know there once was an actual, historical St. Nicholas. We also know he was nothing like the red suited guy who leaves his North Pole toy factory and flies through the air in a sleigh pulled by reindeer every Christmas Eve. The story was just embellished over many years, and just like the gospel accounts of Jesus, there are different versions of his story. I suspect that many children would keep their doubts about Santa to themselves if doubting exposed them not just to the lack of presents, but to the ostracism of their loved ones and the threat of eternal damnation.

Another apologist tactic is to present you with a false choice. They provide a limited number of options, show that one or two of them are highly unlikely, leading to the inevitable conclusion that the only remaining option must be true. The fallacy in their approach is that there are many more options that they never considered or offered as possibilities. For example, they might claim that Jesus was either insane, a liar, or the Son of God. Ruling out insanity and deliberate deception, the only remaining option is that he was the Son of God, which also implies scripture is true, his teachings are true, he is the only way to heaven, etc. The fact is that there are many other possibilities besides the three that the apologist provided you with. One such possibility that many atheists endorse is that there never was a Jesus of Nazareth at all, and the stories about him were composed later for political purposes, or he was actually a literary composite of several different characters. Another possibility is that there was a Jesus, but the stories about what he said and did were embellished and are not historically accurate. Still another possibility is that there was a Jesus who said and believed all of the things he supposedly said and taught, but was simply mistaken. Jesus could have been a charismatic man with devoted followers who believed he was the messiah, and they made the rationalizations necessary to maintain that belief after he was executed. There are many possibilities, but the apologist chooses only two that he feels he can easily discredit, leaving you with only the third possibility, the one he wants you to believe.

Believers often to point to the fact that Old Testament prophecies about the messiah were fulfilled by Jesus, as reported in the New Testament. They sometimes claim that Jesus fulfilled hundreds of biblical prophecies. It's really not necessary to describe and study every single "prophecy" that believers claim was fulfilled by Jesus. There are only three things that you need to know to debunk all of them.

First, the reader may remember the story about the birth of Jesus in Bethlehem, which was added to the gospel to resolve a theological sticking point; Jesus was from Nazareth, but the messiah was to come from Bethlehem. The lesson here, is that if I get to write the story of what happened, I can fulfill any prophecy I want. First century Jews believed the messiah would come from Bethlehem, so when early Christians wrote the story of the person they believed was the messiah, he had to come from Bethlehem, or the Jews they were trying to convince would never believe. So, with the help of a little creative writing, the doubt over a "trivial" detail was erased. Jesus of Nazareth actually was from Bethlehem, doubters just didn't know the whole story.

The second thing you need to know is that if you read many of the Old Testament "prophecies" that Jesus supposedly fulfilled, the texts were not about the messiah at all. Early Christians who felt the Old Testament was prophetic and that Jesus was the messiah, searched for validation of their belief in the Old Testament. When they found something Jesus said, did or had done to him that was mentioned in any context, it was in hindsight, declared a prophecy about the messiah that Jesus fulfilled. That was part of the difficulty early Christians had in winning Jewish converts, as the verses they cited as being fulfilled were not understood to be about the messiah. The messiah was not even mentioned in the text that was "fulfilled". In a similar way, one could take anything that was ever written about death, and pronounce it was a "prophecy" about someone who had died, even though it was not written about the deceased person. The so-called prophecies proving Jesus was the messiah were either stories written about Jesus that were not factual, or Old Testament writings about things that had nothing to do with the messiah.

The third thing you need to know to debunk prophecy is the over-generalized, non-specific prophecy trick. When a prophecy is very general and not specific, almost any event in the world can be viewed as a fulfillment of the "prophecy". The bible tells us that wars, rumors of wars, famine and earthquakes are a sign that the end times are upon us. When, in the history of the mankind, have there not been wars, rumors of war, earthquakes, and famine? Never. So we could also claim that they are signs that the end times are not upon us. Either way, we would be right. Assuming that the world is not eternal and will end sometime, this prophecy about the end times will most certainly be fulfilled, because it lacks any specificity. This type of vagueness is what also allows horoscopes and the prophecies of Nostradamus to "foretell" the future.

I can tell the reader with absolute certainty, that when my words are heeded, there will be great joy in the world. How can I say this with certainty? First, there is always great joy in the world, at least somewhere. I didn't specify that the people who would be joyful would be the same ones who heeded my words, or require a direct causal connection between the heeding of my words and the joy. I also didn't specify which of my words must be heeded to produce the joy. Since I am not the only person in the world who holds my views, it is not even necessary that someone heard of me or my views in order to heed them. They only need to be like-minded in some respect. When phrased with sufficient vagueness and lack of specificity, any "prophecy" made by anyone is certain to be fulfilled.

Apologists sometimes like to ask why the apostles who were martyred for their beliefs would be willing to die in order to defend and promulgate what they knew was actually a lie. The inference is that they wouldn't, which they submit as evidence of the truth of Christianity and that Jesus rose from the dead. The fact that people died for a belief is evidence that the belief was sincerely held, not that it was factual. Throughout history, many people died for beliefs that were not true. Vikings died believing that warriors killed in battle would go to Valhalla. Nazis died for their belief that they were the master race and God was with them. Many people have died by suicide, believing it was the only way to end their emotional pain. Their willingness to die is not evidence that the belief they held was true.

Exactly which of the apostles were martyred? We don't know. There is fairly strong evidence for some (Peter, Paul, and James son of Zebedee and James brother of Jesus) and fairly weak evidence for others, such as John. What is clear, is Christians were persecuted at times and in some cases executed for being Christians. Especially important is exactly what the apostles believed about the resurrection of Jesus. Among the criteria for replacing Judas and becoming an apostle, was a requirement that he had "seen" the risen Lord. Precisely what does that mean?

We know that Paul was considered to have "seen" the risen Lord (1 Cor 15:3-8), even though his experience was a vision which occurred long after Jesus supposedly ascended into heaven. So what exactly did they experience and "see"? Again, we don't know with any reasonable degree of certainty. Perhaps it was nothing more than a rekindled excitement about the teachings of a charismatic dead man who they "felt" was still with them and whose ideas should live on. They may have seen Him in a dream or a vision. Even today many Christians claim to have a personal relationship with Jesus and to communicate with Him, though they don't literally experience His existence with their senses. They "feel" his presence and guidance.

We do know that tales of death and resurrection were common in the ancient world and not unique to Christianity. We also know that many of the stories recorded in the bible were later fabrications that were not believed by the original apostles. Finally, there is no evidence that recanting any specific tenet of the Christian beliefs at the time would have saved them from martyrdom. They were Christians, and that was sufficient basis for their persecution. Early Christians were illiterate people living in an oppressed, occupied country whose religion and cultural identity was threatened. The apostles had met a charismatic man they believed was their messiah, and who they hoped would return to save them. That thin shred of hope in a cruel and hostile world would be lost if they denied Him.

My own skepticism was significantly influenced by the most central claim of Christianity. It is summed up in John 3:16. Obtaining an eternal reward requires you believe Jesus is God, died for your sins and rose from the dead. Some sects differ on the importance or relevance of other things like repentance and good deeds, but faith in Jesus, his divinity and resurrection are core requirements most Christians can agree on. Yet that profession requires faith.

Facts are true regardless of whether or not you believe them. If Jesus died as a human sacrifice to atone for your sins, then the required price has been paid, whether you believe in it or not. Why would God require belief, and particularly belief based on faith? It seems far more plausible to me that belief based on faith was required by early Christians trying to recruit, than by God.

If God really wants all of us to believe something, why doesn't he prove it is true without equivocation? Why hide it in copies of copies of ancient books of dubious reliability? Faith requires belief without evidence, and sometimes despite evidence to the contrary. Yet throughout history, there have been many faiths. If I can't use reason and evidence, how am I, or how is anyone, to decide which faith to accept? The fact is, if you accept Christian dogma, your kind and loving deity will send people to eternal damnation and torment because they didn't guess correctly. People will be condemned for eternity because they were born in the wrong place and culture, where they were incorrectly indoctrinated as children. It doesn't seem fair, does it? It isn't.

Here's another part that doesn't seem fair. Gandhi will be spending eternity in hell, because he didn't have faith in Jesus; Jeffrey Dahmer, a serial killer who repented and was "saved" in prison, will be in heaven. Believe the right stuff just before you die, and you're home free. The worst, most murderous dictators in history can be Jesus' pal in heaven forever, if they just believed the right stuff in time. Either such a deity isn't kind and loving, isn't fair, you mixed up his message, or we should all just listen to our BS detectors. Just believe and have eternal bliss is exactly the same sales pitch Saul of Tarsus used on ancient, ignorant, superstitious people who had no reliable way to discern the truth. While human fears, insecurities and hopes haven't changed since then, our knowledge, and ability to access and evaluate information has changed dramatically.

Superstition and religion are closely intertwined, and the line between them is often blurred. Those who are not Catholic may be unaware of how a statue of St. Joseph can help you sell your house. A practice not officially sanctioned by the church, involves burying a statue of St. Joseph in the yard of the property you have for sale. The exact burial location, direction and depth vary with the source relied upon. However, after closing, the statue is to be dug up and placed on the mantle or similar place of honor in the new home. The practice is supposed to speed the sale of the home as well as increase the price offered for it. The exact origin of this practice is not known, though it appears to be unique to the United States, and became very popular around 1990. Retailers even sell kits, which include a statue, prayer card, and burial instructions. A reasonable question might be whether this is a religious practice or mere superstition, and how to distinguish between the two.

Similarly, Creoles in Louisiana have a number of religious practices that are well beyond official dogma and mix Catholicism with their own culture and traditions. They may involve healers, voodoo specialists, charms, and special saints. Another cultural deviation in religious practice can be seen in the Philippines, where Good Friday is marked by men flogging themselves, with some being crucified, in acts of penance. Culture, superstition and religious practices become intertwined and are often inseparable.

An old truism among debaters is that he who gets to define the terms wins the debate. This is a fact that has not been lost on apologists, who sometimes change the meaning of terms as necessary to suit their argument. It can be very subtle, and if you fail to catch it, their argument can be persuasive. One such apologist argued that space, time and matter had to be created simultaneously by a God who was outside of it, and the bible described that creation accurately in Genesis. In the beginning (time), God created the heavens (space) and the earth (matter). What is the problem here? "In the beginning" is a reference to a point in time when creation began, not to the creation of time itself. The authors of Genesis had no conception of time as it is understood in modern physics. By reinterpreting the meaning of the words, he makes it sound as if they unwittingly stumbled onto it. To the authors of Genesis, the heavens was a physical place above the clouds which was the abode of God. It was most certainly not the equivalent of space as we know it today. Finally, while the earth is made of matter, it is not the definition of matter. There is a lot of matter in the universe, and most of it is not part of earth. Saying God created earth is not the same as saying God created matter, and it is misleading to imply that they are equivalent. Consequently, myths and legends can be construed as scientific fact through the creative redefinition of terms.

I will leave the reader with one final point on the subject of Apologetics. Believers, particularly evangelical believers, like to memorize verses from the bible and can often quote many of them off the top of their head in support of their arguments. Doing so may lend credibility to their point and make it sound more authoritative. However, that approach is really circular reasoning. It is like using the teachings of Buddha to prove that Buddhist practices are wise, or quoting the Quran to prove that the teachings of Islam are correct. A collection of teachings can't be proof of itself. I was once in a discussion with two believers, and one mentioned Psalm 14:1 to the other. That verse is "A fool says in his heart there is no God". In other words, you are a fool if you doubt the things in this document, and I know that is the case because that is one of the sayings in this document. The contents of my book are true because it says so in my book. When challenging someone who doesn't quite grasp the problem with that logic, the reader might counter by quoting Galezewski Chapter 5, final verse: A fool says in his heart there is no God; a wise man says it out loud.

# CHAPTER 6

# The Effects of Religious Belief

> However many holy words you read, however many you
> speak, what good will they do if you do not act on them?
> — **Buddha**

**SOME HAVE ARGUED** that those who are godless are without meaningful controls on their behavior. We need an invisible being in the sky who knows everything we do, and will punish us for infractions even if society doesn't, to keep us in line. It turns out that when you look at the religious beliefs of people in prison, as reported by chaplains in federal and state prisons, their religious beliefs roughly mirror the population of the country as a whole. Criminals by-and-large, are not atheists, and hold more-or-less the same religious beliefs as the rest of us. Admittedly, prisoners may have a motive for lying about their religious faith, there are jailhouse conversions, and just being in prison should convince people to consider a course correction. Still, the evidence does not support that atheism or a lack of faith is at the root of their conduct.

Having religious beliefs is not a sufficient deterrent to keep people from violating our laws. Neither are religious beliefs necessary for people to behave in accord with the norms of society. Netherlands, for example, has a much higher proportion of atheists and agnostics than America, and a much lower crime and incarceration rate. Japan has the highest proportion of convinced atheists in the world, while boasting a crime rate that is among the lowest in the world. We know there are many prominent atheists who were not criminals, and were highly respected members of society. We also know that virtually every law on the books has been broken at one time or another by someone who professed devout religious faith, including members of the clergy. To those who feel they are morally superior to atheists and deserving of heavenly bliss because of their belief in God, I would ask this question: Does Satan believe in God? The answer leads to the unavoidable conclusion that a being can both believe in God, and be the very epitome of evil.

Refraining from bad activities is only one side of the coin. The other is positively engaging in good activities; helping the poor, the suffering, and the sick. Beyond refraining from evil, people do well to act with kindness, empathy, compassion and love. While religions have long encouraged compassion for the less fortunate, is religion or religious belief necessary for people to act compassionately? The evidence from research in the field of psychology is that it is not necessary. It appears that kindness and compassion are instinctive, not only in humans, but other animals as well. Even rats have demonstrated compassion toward a suffering rat and try to help it. Studies on chimpanzees and infants have also supported the instinctive nature of compassion. Children as young as 2 years of age received more happiness from giving treats than from receiving them. Giving is more satisfying in countries around the world, and it holds true whether the nation is rich or poor. One could conclude that "It is more blessed to give than to receive" is more of an observation of intrinsic human nature, than a moral pronouncement.

Not only is God unnecessary for people to behave with compassion, empathy and civility, but religious belief sometimes discourages compassion, empathy and civility. God's law supersedes any man made law, doesn't it? So, once you have determined the will of the Almighty, what is left to discuss? What else matters in determining matters of morality? Nothing. Traditions, cultural norms, compassion, kindness and laws all become meaningless and insignificant when they diverge from what you are sure God wants. That is what makes religious faith so dangerous to orderly, civilized, secular societies that are based on the rule of law. What limit is there on your actions if you are carrying out that which God has ordained? Again, none. The end justifies the means.

Let's look at a few examples. St. Paul used exactly that reasoning in Romans 3:7; the greater moral end justifies lying - which also calls into question whether we can trust anything he wrote. Turn to the Old Testament. Jews believed that the Promised Land was rightfully theirs, promised to them by God. Accordingly, they took it. What limitations were placed on that land acquisition? None. Genocide was ok. Killing every man, woman and child in the way was permissible, even commanded by God, and so done righteously, and with great vigor. Well, except for the occasional virgin, and we all know why they were spared. Fast forward to the Crusades, another holy war slaughtering people in His holy name. If you were a knight and killed in the endeavor, the pope promised you a free ticket straight to heaven. To this day there are lodges that use crusader imagery and terms, thereby elevating the nobility and purpose of their organization, at least in their own minds.

During the Inquisition, all manner of torture and execution was deemed righteous, as it was conducted in the name of God. Some torture devices even had crosses embedded in their design. In early America, innocents accused of being witches were tortured and burned at the stake, justified by a supposed knowledge of God's will. One might wonder how anyone could inflict such suffering on another human who did them no harm and live with themselves, absent heavenly approval.

Latin America speaks Spanish and predominately practices Catholicism, because they were persuaded to do so at the point of a sword by Spanish Catholic conquerors. Native Americans were slaughtered when they stood in the way of "manifest destiny", God's will for America to expand from coast to coast. More recently, America has been on the receiving end of God's will, or at least what some men of faith thought His will was. The 9/11/2001 attack occurred because certain Muslims thought America was evil and that God (Allah) would reward them for sacrificing their own lives by flying a plane into a building, taking 3,000 innocent people with them in the process. ISIS, not unlike ancient Israelites, believed the caliphate was land given to them by God that they were charged with protecting for future generations of Muslims. During World War II, Germany's Wehrmacht used *Gott mit uns* (God with us) as a slogan to legitimize their cause. Hitler himself proclaimed that his was a Christian movement.

Religion has justified criminalizing homosexuality and denying them the same rights other citizens enjoy. Religion has even provided some people with the justification necessary to bomb abortion clinics and murder physicians who perform abortions. Christianity has historically blamed people of Jewish heritage for the death of Jesus (Matt 27:25) and treated them accordingly. In March of 2021, a young man entered three different spas near Atlanta and murdered 8 women inside. The gunman was both religious and a sex addict, who had been a patient in an evangelical treatment center. He felt these spas, and apparently their employees, were a source of temptation that he needed to eliminate. Finally, consider the barbaric public canings and beheadings regularly carried out in Saudi Arabia, often for religious dissent or violating religious dogma. As Steven Weinberg famously said, "With or without religion, good people can behave well and bad people can do evil; but for good people to do evil, that takes religion".

One might argue that those who harm others in the name of their religion or do what anyone with a sense of compassion would regard as evil have misinterpreted their faith. They don't understand the teachings or the scripture correctly. Perhaps that is true. But who is to say what the correct interpretation is with authority? Many hundreds, perhaps thousands of people have claimed that authority and that insight, all the while contradicting each other, even starting their own religious sects. They had visions, messages from above, and prayerful insights that told them they were on the right path, and those who disagreed were wrong. They had a lineage from the originator of the faith that the others lack, while disagreeing on what the "true" lineage is or who may have departed from it. Yet their faiths riddled them with guilt over their natural sexual urges, convinced them of their sinful nature and worthlessness. Their dogma held that women are lesser human beings than men, taught them to scorn non believers, and to segregate themselves from humans who had different beliefs. They believed that taking up the sword against infidels and pagans was righteous. Even if it were true that they were wrong in their interpretation of their religion and scripture, how could you possibly prevent unorthodox or heretical religious beliefs from being held? They tried with great vigor during the inquisitions, and failed miserably.

As I write this, America is in the midst of a global pandemic caused by the Covid-19 virus. At this moment, some 65,000 people have died from it in the United States alone, and public health experts have predicted the death toll could exceed 200,000. That number, though shocking and alarming, later proved to be extremely optimistic. Throughout the country, people have been encouraged to stay home except when necessary to get food or medication, or to work in an essential occupation. In many states, that has been required by law. Schools are closed and large public gatherings are prohibited. No concerts, no sporting events, no church. Pastors in Florida, Louisiana and Texas continued to hold services with large gatherings, despite the danger that posed to their flock, as well as other people those church members later came in contact with. A Catholic Cardinal (Burke) in Italy, declared that they are not subject to such prohibitions by civil authorities and that church attendance is more important than the risk to public health. Some Muslims have declared that, contrary to the evidence, only infidels are infected by the virus and they continue gathering in mosques, believing they are protected from the virus by Allah. Once people determined the will of God in the matter, no law, no science, no reason, no threat to public health, no number of deaths, was relevant.

I would be remiss if I failed to mention that barbaric cruelty and evil, historically characteristic of Abrahamic religions, is not universal in all religions. Pastafarianism, America's fastest growing carbohydrate based faith, includes no such practices. In fact, in all of recorded history, not a single person has been harmed in the name of their deity, the Flying Spaghetti Monster (FSM). I felt this important to point out, because people sometimes judge the validity of religious teaching by its fruits.

All of that is not to say Abrahamic religions are purely evil. Many religions and churches do lots of kind, charitable things that we all support, even if we reject the underlying doctrine. For example, many hospitals and orphanages were founded by religious organizations, albeit with other people's money and a golden opportunity to proselytize and support the members of their religious order. It is to say that religion and religious authority has been, and still is, used to justify all manner of foolishness, cruelty and inhumanity. Atheists, such as Stalin, may do things that are immoral and abhorrent, but they make no claims of supernatural authority or justification for their deeds. The Bible teaches us that Abraham was holy, righteous and good, because he was willing to murder his own son to please God. Murdering an innocent child under any circumstance doesn't even approach good on my moral compass, or that of most people. Only a deity could interject a sense of righteousness into such an act. There is no cruelty, no inhumanity, nothing that is immoral, when commanded or approved of by God. Religion is a catalyst that ennobles, invigorates and adds fuel to the fire of cruelty that innocent people have literally been thrown into. As Pascal wrote, "Men never do evil so completely and cheerfully as when they do it from religious conviction".

I previously mentioned the words of Dostoyevsky, that without God, all things are permitted. There is an upside to all things being permitted if there is no God prohibiting them. The upside is this: we no longer have to obey the ancient edicts recorded by ignorant, superstitious, misogynist men who claimed they had discerned God's will. We are free to decide how our society should work, how much freedom of choice can be allowed, what behavior should be sanctioned, and how it should be sanctioned. We can rely on medical, psychological, sociological and other scientific evidence in making those decisions. What actually works can replace what heaven supposedly commanded. Decisions can be based on evidence rather than disputed claims of authority. We can organize and run our society on the basis of what we know, rather than what we have faith in. It's hard for some Americans to believe and may feel disloyal to acknowledge, but some countries have solved many of the social problems we are still grappling with by using that approach.

There are those who would argue "Science" is defective and should not be used in making societal decisions. The defect is that it assumes and looks only for "natural" explanations, without even considering the possibility that supernatural explanations could be correct. I would counter that the proof is in the pudding. Which explanatory method has consistently produced useful, verifiable results – science, or religious dogma?

Those who came up with the germ theory of illness completely ignored the explanation that plagues and other illnesses were caused by sin. The scientific approach produced vaccines, which actually prevented illness, even among the sinful. While scientific explanations for illness produced antibiotics that cured the sick, supernatural explanations produced burned offerings, prayer, penance, suffering and death. Scientists never seriously considered the possibility that epileptic seizures could be caused by evil spirits or demonic possession, instead, opting for biological and electro-chemical explanations involving the brain. Instead of exorcisms, they produced medications and surgical interventions that stopped or reduced the frequency of the seizures. When exploring why people don't fly off into space, science came up with "gravity". They never even considered the possibility that the Flying Spaghetti Monster is invisibly holding us down with his noodley appendages.

Science always ignores supernatural explanations that can't be tested or proven true or false, and the benefits of that approach are indisputable. One of the reasons scientists became so excited about the Higgs boson discovery, (the so-called "God particle") is that with it, they discovered everything that significantly affects the physical world we live in. There is no mechanism left by which spirits, prayers, demons, telepathy, witchcraft, angels, voodoo, curses or karma can have any effect on our physical world. Some might term such claims blasphemy or heresy, terms that only mean the evidence you speak of contradicts religious dogma, and so must be silenced. Science, in contrast, places no such stigma on any evidence. The facts and the evidence reveal what they reveal, regardless of how you feel about it or what other things you believe. Fact is neither good nor evil, it is only factual.

Another effect of religious belief is that it provides comfort and hope to people during trying times. A loved one who died will be missed, but only for a time. They are in a better place, and you have hope that one day, you will be reunited. I encountered a high school classmate at a social function who I hadn't seen in many years, and learned he had a son who drowned in a tragic accident. One of his comments to me was that people without God in that circumstance are left with no hope. He clung to the hope of being reunited with his son some day, and didn't know how he could bear his grief without it. I have two other friends who both lost a child unexpectedly under tragic circumstances. Neither felt they could have survived the experience without the hope that they had from their religious beliefs. When you suffer another type of loss, perhaps a job or a marriage, there is some solace in believing that there is an invisible friend who is powerful, loves you, will watch out for you, and help see you through it. Suffering, and sometimes the status quo that produced it, is endured because it happens for a reason, and that reason is to eventually produce a better outcome for you. Not only is suffering purposeful, you will eventually go to an even greater reward, and unlike your current suffering, the reward will last forever.

I would compare the comfort of religious belief to a purely secular experience of my own. After a couple years as a police officer, I saw more violence, dishonesty and rottenness than I ever could have imagined existed in the world. Then we took a vacation to Disney World. For the time we were there, I did not hear so much as one cross word spoken by anyone. Everywhere you looked, smiling children, singing, music, beautiful flowers, pleasant and helpful staff and amazing attractions. Disney World was the perfect prescription for recharging my psychological batteries, but it would be foolish to live there. Why? Because it isn't real. It is a very expensive, very well-orchestrated, fantasy. It *is* a magic kingdom, and there is good reason not to live in a world of fantasy and magic, no matter how good it makes you feel.

We all know about churches that teach believers can handle deadly snakes without harm based on Mark 16:18, incorporating that practice into their services. Sadly, every now and then, we read a story about how the snake won, on occasion killing someone who was so certain God would save them, that they refused medical help. The same verse also says they will also drink deadly poison without harm, though as far as I know, they haven't worked that part into their services. Well, except for Jonestown, and we all know how that turned out. So even they have limits on how far to take the fantasy. More often than we should, we read about the parents of a sick child who determined the child would be healed with prayer and medical attention withheld, demonstrating the strength of their faith, only to have the child die. I once had a chat with a man who wanted to retire but couldn't afford to because of the cost of his wife's medications, though he didn't mention the nature of her illness or the specific medications. They discussed the matter, prayed about it, and decided to "put her in the lord's hands". She stopped her medications and he retired. That's the place that living in the fantasy takes you to; recklessly denying reality, and ignoring the evidence you wish wasn't there.

One of the most distressing feelings we can have in life is helplessness. If you have watched the suffering of a dying loved one, you know how painful the resulting emotions are. No matter how much you want to change things, you can't heal their affliction or ease their suffering. You are indeed helpless. Yet with religion, that feeling of helplessness is eased. There is something you can do – pray. Ask an invisible deity to ease their suffering, or provide an impossible and miraculous cure. Perhaps offer a bargain promising what you will do in return if your wish is fulfilled. You might even ask to take their place and endure the pain yourself to relieve their suffering. The feeling of control you might receive from such prayer is only a combination of wishful thinking and self-deception.

Prayer has been researched: it doesn't work. Here's how we know. A number of hospitalized sick people had congregations pray for their recovery, while other hospitalized patients with similar conditions did without the prayer. The ones who were prayed for didn't do any better, and actually did a little worse. No higher recovery rate, no speedier recovery, no fewer complications, no nothing. I know the Bible demands you are not to test God. If I proclaimed a falsehood was true, I wouldn't want it tested either. But that directive was composed long before randomized experiments with experimental and control groups and tests of statistical significance were even invented; so it's safe to say scientific experiments are not the kind of test the biblical directive was referring to.

In the context of this discussion, the reader might consider the number of people on earth who have died. Current estimates are that somewhere around 100 billion humans have lived on earth. With the exception of the people alive today (about 7.9 billion of us), all of those many billions of people have died. Imagine the number of prayers said beseeching a deity to intervene and spare the life of the deceased, both their own prayers and those of loved ones. I think it's safe to say that over the span of human existence, every God ever believed in and worshipped by humans has been begged, implored, sacrificed to, and bargained with to spare a human life. Every ritual, prayer, blessing and incantation, ever created has been tried in an effort to stop someone from dying. These supplications have been undertaken by people regarded as holy, evil, and every degree of righteousness in between. Some were rich, some poor, some well educated, some illiterate, some powerful and some powerless. Yet all of those prayers went unanswered. Every single one of those people who were prayed for, died. In all of history, all of those prayers to all of those deities were for naught. That's not to say that sick people never recover from illness, but the dying die, and one day we will all be there, no matter the futile efforts of the faithful. The fact that their prayers have failed 100 billion times is pretty compelling evidence it doesn't work.

Things change when we do something to change them. Prayer may make you feel better about the situation, but it does nothing to change it. Every mass shooting produces "thoughts and prayers" but no meaningful action, until the next one, when we think and pray some more. That is the danger of the fantasy. Wait for the invisible deity to fix it for you, relieving you of the necessity of taking any action, all the while feeling that you did something. A few dollars to support medical research does more to cure an illness than all the prayers and burned incense in all of the world's churches. Without a hereafter to enjoy, there is an urgency to solving our problems now, rather than quietly and prayerfully enduring them until our afterlife begins.

Admittedly, it is true that sometimes, the thing people pray for occurs: a sick person recovers, someone got the job they wanted, or conceived and successfully delivered the baby they had long hoped for. It is also true that sometimes, the same results are obtained through lucky rabbits feet, four leaf clovers, and wishing on a star. The only difference is that in the latter cases, most people recognize the connection between the outcome and the presumed cause as mere superstition.

Consider the psychology of the prayerful. No matter what the outcome, whether or not it was what they prayed for, in their minds, the prayer was answered. Pray for someone who makes a complete recovery, and it is proof that God is good and answered your prayers. A miracle. If they survive with extensive disability, their survival is an answered prayer, proof that He is good, and some greater good or lesson will result from this disability, even though we don't know what it is. If the person dies, God works in ways beyond our understanding, and the suffering of the deceased is over, proof that God is good and answers prayer, even if not in the precise way we had hoped. Their belief can't be falsified. You could produce exactly the same result by praying to a telephone pole. Sometimes they recover completely, sometimes partially, sometimes they die, and each of the outcomes occurs in the same proportion of cases whether we rely on God, the telephone pole, or the rabbit's foot. While prayer does not alter the outcome, it does give the person who prayed three things; a convoluted and fabricated explanation for the outcome, a sense of control over an event that they really had no control over, and a false reason to hope.

Believers often fail to consider the relationship between prayer and the divine plan that they often assert God has for their lives. If He has a plan which is the best outcome possible for you, as many believers assert, why ask him for anything at all? If it's part of His plan, it will happen without praying. Just get out of the way and let His plan unfold. Why would you risk praying for some outcome that might not be part of His perfect plan? What if He were to approve your foolish request? Do you think your plan is better than His? Put another way, the late Christopher Hitchens once said that the man who prays thinks his deity has it all wrong, but that he can instruct Him on how to set it right.

I think every reasonably intelligent person knows that their chance of winning the lottery is minuscule. Yet every year or so, when I happen to see some news story that the jackpot is very large, I will buy a ticket. Why throw my money away? Because for a couple bucks, I can spend all the free time I have imagining what I would do with all that money if I won. It's fantasy, no real harm, and it brings me some enjoyment to dream about what I would do if I won $500 million. To me, the ticket is cheap entertainment that you can buy for only $2. Importantly, I don't live in that fantasy, while some people do. Especially people who are poor, don't handle money well, and are banking on it to solve their financial woes. They play it often, sometimes every drawing, and often buy a lot more than one ticket. They are living in the fantasy. There are other things that are much more likely to straighten out their finances: a personal finance class, budgeting, paying off high interest debt, perhaps a part time job, or career move to boost their income. Not only are they failing to do things that could help, but living in the fantasy actually hurts; the money they are losing on the lottery is wasted, making their financial condition worse than it was before. In that same way, enduring hardship and suffering in anticipation of a big payout when we die, only guarantees continued hardship and suffering in this life, the only one we are certain to have.

A positive benefit of religious belief is absolution from guilt. Probably every human who has lived has done something they later regretted and wished they could take back. Sometimes they didn't take time to evaluate whether it was right, or were overcome with emotions that they acted on. Sometimes they knew it was wrong, but lust, greed, or other desire had a stronger influence on their behavior than their conscience. Guilt and shame can haunt us and keep us from moving forward. Sometimes, people are driven to suicide to escape these powerful feelings. Often, adverse events in life that we bear no responsibility for cause us to wonder what we might have done wrong or how we could have prevented them from occurring. Survivors of a loved one's suicide, for example, often second-guess and blame themselves, wondering what they did wrong, what they could have done differently, what they missed, and in so doing, torment themselves.

Whatever action or inaction we may feel guilt over, religion absolves us of guilt, assures us we have been forgiven, and gives us a path forward. The Jewish temple of the first century was a sacrificial factory in which animals of various types were continuously slaughtered and burned to make amends with God. They even made daily sacrifices on behalf of the Roman emperor, which was part of their deal with Rome for allowing them to continue their religious practices. Jesus was a sacrifice on behalf of all believers, for the forgiveness of sin. Sacrifice and forgiveness have long been an integral part of religious beliefs. I may have been wrong, made mistakes, harmed others, or harmed society, but am forgiven. I have a fresh start. No longer need to carry the guilt and shame. I am born again, saved, redeemed.

The assertion is sometimes made by the faithful that religion gives mankind the answers to the most important questions of life, which science is unable to do. Questions like "What is the purpose and meaning of my life?" OK, that's a little like saying science can't answer the really important questions, like "How many fairies can fit inside of a 16 oz. glass jar?" First, the importance of any question is a matter of opinion. Second, science can't answer questions that are based on a false premise. Since fairies don't exist, there is no measurement of their size or mass, and science can't tell you how many would fit in a 16 oz. jar. Only fairy tales could answer such a question.

Similarly, science can't tell you your purpose, because the question itself presupposes that there is a purpose and meaning for your life. What evidence is there that any of us have some important purpose and significance or that there is some great, divine play we have a lead role in? The grim truth is, most of us go through a period of development, we love and are loved, we work, reproduce, grow old, and die. A hundred years after we die, the world is no better or worse for most of us having been in it. Like your family dog, you may have brought someone some happiness or comfort, but neither of you played any discernible role in any grand, divine plan. We like to think that we hold a special place in the universe, yet science and evidence tells us we aren't all that special. Humans are unique in our ability to speak, yet many animals and even trees communicate with each other. We have feelings and emotions, but so do lots of animals. We think and reason, but are not really all that good at it. We are special and important to the universe only in our own estimation.

There is no objective reason to believe your life has some noble, invaluable purpose, which is precisely why science can't tell you what it is. Your life has the purpose you give it. That purpose might be making as much money as possible, experiencing as much pleasure and as little pain as you can, charitably helping others and improving their lot in life, acquiring as much power as possible, bringing joy to others through your talent in the arts, doing everything possible to help guide and support your family, or something else, likely multiple purposes. Purpose doesn't come from some invisible being that exists somewhere outside of space and time. Those who "need" an answer to a nonsensical question find it in myth, legend, fable and superstition of necessity; such answers don't exist in reality. The sense of purpose and meaning one may feel from religious faith affirms your worth, value and importance. It feels good and feeds your self esteem, whether it is true or not. Emotions are often more persuasive and compelling than facts and evidence. That, in part, is why we are not all that good at reasoning.

Another effect of religious belief is that the clergy who lead the faithful often provide advice and counseling that people find helpful. As a police officer, I often encountered people in crisis. They experienced serious emotional situations that overwhelmed their ability to think rationally. Someone died, cheated on them, insulted them, beat them up, or otherwise evoked an emotional response that overwhelmed any rational thought. I reached two conclusions after witnessing this regularly for years, meeting people at some of the worst times of their lives: first, emotion trumps reason every time. Second, in those horrible, trying, difficult times, we need someone else to do our thinking for us, or at least help us with the process, because we can't think straight. We need someone to tell us we are on the wrong track, to steer us and help us through the problem by following a reasonable path. Little wonder then, that people who commit the most notorious, despicable crimes are often described as loners; they had no one to help steer them on a reasonable course, tell them they were headed the wrong way, and were left to their own devices. Long before police, psychologists or social workers, people turned to religious leaders as the source they could trust for that kind of help, guidance and direction.

Of course, religious authorities are people too, and so that trust has sometimes been misplaced. One such example is in my wife's family lore. Her maternal grandfather was a community leader in Poland who disassociated himself from the church. The separation occurred because the local priest advised a widow who had a cow (and depended on it to support her children), to sell it and donate the proceeds to the church. Nonetheless, religious authorities are often sought out to this day for their advice and counsel in a wide variety of matters. They often discuss problems in confidence and free of charge, no health insurance or deductibles necessary. Clergy are often more educated than their followers, looked up to in the community, respected and readily accessible. They often have some training in psychology and counseling.

Clergy usually have a genuine concern for other people and their well being. For those reasons their counsel is often sought, and is often helpful.

The last effect of religious belief, or more specifically Judeo-Christian religious belief, that I will consider here, is dominion. The Bible teaches us that mankind has dominion over the earth and its flora and fauna. While theologians argue over the correct interpretation of "dominion", the practical interpretation, the one Christians have acted on for centuries, is that it's all here to serve us, to meet our needs and desires. We use it as we choose, and have divine license to do so. In the thousands of years since the words that gave man dominion were written, we have learned a lot. We learned about eco-systems, their various components, and how important all of those pieces are. No one piece is there solely to serve or be served by the others. They are all interconnected and interdependent. Stress any part, and all the other parts share the adverse effects.

This religious doctrine of man having dominion over the earth has produced immense harm to the environment, the extinction of species, the pollution of our air and water, decimation of the world's rain forests, and contributed to the problem of climate change. All of this damage was done with the belief it was ok, because God said so. Dog fighting, bull fighting and trophy hunting are not only barbaric cruelties, they are affirmed by the belief that the other sentient beings on earth exist only for our pleasure and to serve us. Dominion over the earth is a dangerous principle, rooted in religion, which gave man license to damage this planet in ways it, and we, may never fully recover from.

# Religious Influence on American Politics

> It is a truism that almost any sect, cult, or religion will legislate its creed into law if it acquires the political power to do so.
>
> — <u>Robert A. Heinlein</u>

**A FEW YEARS** ago, I was having a discussion with a friend about elections and election ads. My complaint was that they did little or nothing to educate or inform voters, and often misled and misinformed the electorate. He shared an insight I have not forgotten; elections, election campaigns and election ads are not about informing or educating – they are about marketing. The goal is not to inform the electorate of your position and the reasons that position makes the most sense. The goal is to get people to buy what you are selling; to create a positive, favorable impression of your candidate, and an unfavorable impression of the opposition. How many times have you heard someone say they like or don't like a particular candidate, while they knew little or nothing about their policy positions? That is the power of marketing and how elections are won or lost in 21st century America. Hundreds of millions of dollars are spent on these marketing campaigns, often funded by people whose identities and purpose are concealed from the rest of us.

In this political environment, reason, logic and facts only play a bit part in the eventual outcome. Facts have become indistinguishable from opinions in the political arena. Gaslighting is a term and a practice often used in politics. It refers to a tactic of deception that employs repeated lying, denial, misdirection and obfuscation. Its ultimate goal is to undermine a person's confidence in their ability to distinguish between fact and fiction, truth and falsehood, making them dependent on an individual or source to make that determination for them. Adding to the confusion is the many, often contradictory, sources of news and information readily available to the general public. The landscape has changed markedly from the era of three news networks with a fairness doctrine that was imposed by the FCC. With cable, streaming and the internet, we are awash in news sources. Some freely mix news and opinion, some sources specialize in satire, and some lack journalistic integrity, publishing information that has not been verified as accurate in their haste to "scoop" the competition. Little wonder then, that many people don't know who to believe.

In America today, it seems that everything has become political and a matter of opinion, including matters of science. For example, the question of whether the climate is warming, the rate of the change, and the cause of the change, are empirical, scientific questions, not matters of opinion. How we should respond to the evidence, what actions we should take, are legitimate political questions about which reasonable people can disagree, but not the scientific evidence itself. That is a question of fact, data and evidence, not political opinion. Yet in America today, what is factual has been turned into a political debate.

In the same way, COVID 19 has become a political issue rather than a matter of facts, data and evidence. The balancing of public health and the economic impact of specific measures are legitimate political topics and resolved in the political arena. The illness itself, its effects on the population, treatments and the effectiveness of protective measures are scientific questions that are being answered, often erroneously, by politicians. A general lack of trust in anything we are told by anyone exacerbates the problem, and contributes to wild conspiracy theories that many accept as factual, even without any supporting evidence.

Perhaps it is no surprise then, that in a murky world where facts and opinions, truth and falsehood are intermingled, religion has sought to enhance its influence. In a world of confusion and uncertainty, it provides many with an anchor of certainty in the shifting tides of public sentiment.

For decades, Christians, particularly evangelicals prevalent in America's Bible Belt, have been trying to weave their religious views into the fabric of our society through active participation in the political process. The issues of primary concern to them seem to be abortion, homosexuality, and matters that involve separation of church and state, at least when the separation involves their church. For example, they object to the prohibition on public school authorities leading students in prayer. I believe I am correct in asserting that Christian parents would object to similar prayer led by public school teachers, but directed to Allah or Vishnu. They also object to prohibitions against Christian symbols (e.g. a nativity scene) being displayed on public property, as they are an endorsement of a particular religious faith by government. Again, they almost certainly would object to symbols that are used by other faiths being displayed on government property. So it is really only the separation between the state and *their* religion that they object to.

Special treatment, they feel, should be afforded to them, because we are a Christian nation, founded by Christians. That position requires a distorted view of history. First, we are only a Christian nation in the sense that it is the most widely practiced religion. Yet nothing in our founding documents prescribes Christianity as the official faith, or limited freedom of religion to choosing between Christian sects. Quite the contrary, the constitution prohibits the establishment of an official religion or favoring any religion over the others. While many of America's founding fathers were Christians, some were not. Washington and Jefferson, for example, were Deists. Ben Franklin was arguably a man of no real religious faith at all. These men of prominence aside, we had Jews living in America since the 1600's. Native Americans had their own spiritual beliefs and were not Christians until compelled to be. Similarly, Black slaves were not Christians until compelled to be. So the Christian argument for special consideration is based on the fact that they share a variant of the faith that some, but not all, of the white male Europeans of prominence held at the time America was founded. Yet those founders didn't think Christianity important enough to even mention when they drafted the foundational document of our government, the constitution.

We all have a sense of morality, of what is good, and bad, of what is fair and unfair. We inevitably take that sense of morality with us into the voting booth. The collective outcome is reflected in our laws. In the end, all of our laws are held to another standard, the constitution. It is the measure by which all laws are judged and a determination is made whether the law shall be allowed to stand. Public sentiment and the will of the electorate are subordinate to the constitution itself. The evangelical right has long been attempting to thwart that constitutional protection and impose their religious view as the final determinant of law in America. That includes issues ranging from what is taught and who is prayed to in public schools, what is displayed on public property, the treatment of homosexuals and whether or under what circumstances women have a right to abortion. Laws such as "continuity of care" for abortion providers and providing unnecessary procedures prior to performing an abortion have nothing to do with concern for the health of women. They are thinly veiled efforts to impose their religious belief about abortion on other people, making what the courts have deemed a right as difficult as possible to exercise.

America was formed as a country governed by well intentioned people, whose morality would inform their judgments in civic affairs; not humans acting with divine certainty that they could impose on their fellow countrymen. A peculiar logic has arisen in America, by which treating all other people equally has been dubbed discrimination against religious liberty. This is a pernicious effort to make evangelical religious views favored and protected by law. The claim has been made by a clerk who refused to issue a marriage license to a gay couple, and a baker who refused to make a cake for one. In essence, they refused to do their job when it required them to provide a service to gay people, and then claimed doing so would somehow victimize them.

They assert that prohibiting me from discriminating against people who don't live by my faith is discriminating against me. Imagine a Catholic pharmacist who refused to fill a birth control prescription, a Baptist store clerk who refused to scan your beer at the checkout, a Lutheran firefighter who refused to work on Sundays because it is the Sabbath, or a Muslim photographer who refused to take fashion photos because the models were not wearing a hijab. More recently in Montana, the claim was made when tax credits for scholarships to religious schools were deemed to be prohibited under their state constitution. Nobody prohibited anyone from going to any religious school, but the plaintiffs claimed discrimination against her religious freedom, because the state wouldn't use tax dollars to pay for her religious choice.

A country of people with different faiths, each acting on behalf of a God who gives them different directions which supersede any man made law, is doomed to unending conflict, violence, and ultimately, failure. Look no further than the Middle East, where Sunni and Shiite Muslims are continuously killing each other. History is replete with such examples of violent religious conflict. It is exactly such conflict that America's founders sought to avoid. As James Madison wrote, "The purpose of separation of church and state is to keep forever from these shores the ceaseless strife that has soaked the soil of Europe in blood for centuries".

Barry Goldwater, a conservative US Senator and Republican nominee for president in 1964, warned about the problem posed when religion and politics become so intertwined. "Mark my word; if and when these preachers get control of the [Republican] party, and they're sure trying to do so, it's going to be a terrible damn problem. Frankly, these people frighten me. Politics and governing demand compromise. But these Christians believe they are acting in the name of God, so they can't and won't compromise. I know, I've tried to deal with them." As I have pointed out repeatedly, when you have determined the will of the Almighty on an issue, there is no room left for discussion or compromise. They would be ecstatic if America were to become a Christian theocracy and are slowly working toward that end. Yet much of world was ruled by Christian theocracy before. We now call that time the Dark Ages.

Evangelical Christians have closely aligned themselves with the Republican Party. Most recently, President Trump has had their overwhelming support. Let's consider some of the actions and positions of conservative Republicans. Refugees were fleeing out of control crime and violence in Central America, and coming to the United States, among other countries. The conservative solution is to build a wall to keep them out, and to imprison those who try to get in. Tax policy has been to cut taxes in a way that provided the biggest benefit to large corporations and those who are already wealthy. Healthcare efforts have been limited to sabotaging Obamacare, resulting in the loss of health insurance for millions of people, most of limited means. Looking at the financial position of the working poor, real wages, adjusted for inflation, were the same in 2020 as they were in 1973. The federal minimum wage remains unchanged. Their 2020 budget proposed cutting spending on Medicare, Medicaid and Social Security, programs that primarily benefit the poor and elderly. The stock market was doing well until the corona virus pandemic, but that wealth was only received by people who already had sufficient disposable income to invest in the stock market. 45% of Americans did not share in that bounty.

The differences between these policies and the spirit of Jesus' teachings are stark. By that I don't mean the Republican Evangelical or the prosperity gospel versions of Jesus, I mean the original. The Jesus who advised you to sell all you have and give it to the poor, which would produce treasure in heaven. The Jesus who asked how God's love could abide in a man who closed his heart to a brother in need. The one who said he who has two tunics should share with another who has none. The one who, in Matthew 25:34-40, who told us to welcome strangers, clothe the naked, care for the sick and imprisoned. The one who said it is easier for a camel to pass through the eye of a needle than for a rich man to get to heaven. Evangelicals don't want these teachings to be part of how we decide to be governed. As the late George Carlin quipped, the people who always ask "what would Jesus do?" don't want to know so they can do it. They want to know, so they know what to tell you that you should do. Like Pharisees, they memorize verses, preach God's commands and sit in judgment others, all the while overlooking the spirit of the teachings they profess to believe. It seems our personal financial interests and economic status can have a dramatic effect on our interpretation of scripture.

I close this chapter with a quotation I came across from Chris Hedges. "And what I'm willing to do, which the mainstream church is not, is to denounce the Christian Right as Christian heretics. You don't have to, as I did, spend three years at Harvard Divinity School to realize that Jesus didn't come to make us rich. And he certainly didn't come to make Pat Robertson and Joel Osteen rich. And what they have done is acculturate the worst aspects of American imperialism, capitalism, chauvinism, violence and bigotry into the Christian religion."

# CHAPTER 8

# Conclusion

> The opinions that are held with passion are always those
> for which no good ground exists; indeed the passion is the
> measure of the holder's lack of rational conviction. Opinions
> in politics and religion are almost always held passionately.
> — **Bertrand Russell**

**AT THIS POINT,** I expect that the reader will be wondering how people could possibly be so foolish and believe the idiotic things they do. Some readers will ask that about the religious, while others will ask that about me. It is an interesting question, one I hope to provide some insight into. I hope that some understanding will help temper the passion with which we hold our views, and facilitate finding a way we can live together even with our differences.

There is a demand often made in America today, that you must respect the religious beliefs of others. I vehemently maintain that you don't. Beliefs aren't entitled to respect. Beliefs are rightly subject to scrutiny, argument, evaluation, skepticism, critical evaluation, and sometimes, contempt. Beliefs are always subordinate to the facts and evidence that bear on them. It doesn't matter whether the beliefs are about religion, politics, physics or medicine. People must be respected if we are to get along and reach a consensus, and the right to hold and express one's beliefs must be respected for the same reason. However, the beliefs and ideas themselves are entitled to no special exemption from scrutiny or opposition and are not inherently deserving of respect, even when they claim to have divine origin. Many mutually exclusive beliefs make that claim, making it clear that some must be false. Some ideas and beliefs are foolish, dangerous, harmful, or just not factual, and unworthy of respect for those reasons. Discussions of what beliefs are right and supported by the evidence, are more fruitful than arguments over what person, political party or religion is right. Every person, political party and religion is wrong, at least sometimes, on some matters. Infallibility is not a trait found in Homo Sapiens.

Scientists who study human cognition have long been aware of the fact that we are not all that logical and rational in our views, and they have demonstrated that experimentally many times. Oh, we are very good at finding all the errors and logical fallacies in the arguments made by those we disagree with; we just don't see the error in our own positions with equal clarity. In addition to the errors we make in objectively evaluating facts and fairly weighing the evidence, people are tribal by nature and often adopt the views of other members of their group, even though they may know very little about the topic themselves. For example, if you believe government restrictions on the movements and activities of healthy people during the Covid–19 pandemic were excessive or unconstitutional, you are probably also pro-life, opposed to government restrictions on gun ownership, oppose legalizing recreational cannabis, and believe man-made climate change is not an imminent threat to humanity. People who disagree on one of these issues likely disagree on all or most of them, even though the issues themselves are completely unrelated to each other, as are the relevant facts. We tend to agree with other members of our "tribe", and don't need a lot of solid evidence to do so, often just trusting in the assessment made by other members of the group we identify with.

The Tea Party movement is an excellent example of an effort to promote ideological purity within the "tribe". Conservatives who were not in agreement with them on all the issues of the day were deemed a RINO (Republican In Name Only), renounced as "not a true conservative", or worse yet, a "libtard". Being "one of us" required agreement on multiple, unrelated issues. Liberal Democrats put forward similar calls for ideological purity in the 2020 election, referring to party members who do not share their views as "corporate Democrats" and "Republican light". In both cases, the effort is directed toward defining the "tribe" by its beliefs and discouraging dissent, bringing members into lockstep on a variety of issues. In both cases, it is also an effort to move the party to the more extreme fringes. Compromise is unacceptable, because it only benefits "them". The message is clear; if you want to be one of "us", get on board with the program. The group defines who "we" are, and a lack of ideological purity means you are not worthy of the title the rest of the group enjoys.

You may have shared my experience of pointing to data supporting your position, only to be told that "people can use statistics to prove anything they want" as they dismiss the evidence before their eyes. The data itself doesn't have to be inaccurate or misinterpreted to be discounted this way. They just found a catch phrase that allows them to conveniently dismiss any quantitative evidence that conflicts with the views they already hold. That is certainly easier than thoughtfully evaluating the data and re-evaluating our views if the data is accurate and correctly interpreted. Most of us tend to follow this easier path. If you were wrong about one thing, you could have been wrong about others, and would have to revise the whole paradigm that you use to make sense of the world. That paradigm was built over many years of learning and through experiences that we don't dismiss lightly. Changing it requires a lot of work to resolve all of the potential conflicting facts and beliefs, because after many years, most of the things that you hold to be true have become intricately intertwined.

I have a friend who once told me there is evidence for every viewpoint people hold, but he has certain core beliefs that he goes to that help him clear up the ambiguity. Put another way, he has an ideology that filters which facts to believe. Those that are in concert with his ideology are true, and the rest can safely be dismissed as false. Psychologists call that *confirmation bias*. We readily accept as factual information that confirms what we already believe, and reject information that calls our beliefs into question. In recent times, the phrase "fake news" has been routinely used to dismiss information that is inconsistent with a person's beliefs, even when the information before them is neither fake, nor news. It is the adult equivalent of putting your fingers in your ears while shouting "Na na na na". Regardless of our political leanings, when encountering information that is in conflict with what we believe, our first inclination is to dismiss the information. It is simply the way our human brains work.

Oftentimes, very smart people suspend their critical thinking or don't delve deeply enough into the subject. After all, we can't all be experts on everything, and we sometimes just trust other people who have what we regard as expertise. Many atheists and agnostics have made the claim that theists must be stupid to believe things that anyone with an ounce of sense should be able to see are nonsense. Nothing could be further from the truth. Many religious people are very smart, but they adopted their religious beliefs for reasons that have little or nothing to do with their intellect. Once their beliefs were adopted, their intellect serves to help them explain and defend their chosen set of beliefs.

I think the key distinction between believers and non believers is not intellect, but the quantity and strength of evidence they require to accept religious claims. Faith is not a decision on which side of the scale of evidence is heaviest. It is a decision of whether the evidence is good enough for you. I previously mentioned the Carl Sagan quote "Extraordinary claims require extraordinary evidence". For him, the evidence supporting religious belief was never good enough, never reached his required threshold. In contrast, someone once told me that they believed in the bodily resurrection of Jesus from the dead, because that is the most plausible explanation for the evidence that exists. The bodily resurrection of a dead person has never been reliably reported or observed by anyone who is alive today, although it was frequently reported to have occurred in the first century. Such an event is impossible according to the laws of science. Yet they consider it more plausible than any other possible explanation. Looking at it objectively, any explanation that is even remotely possible is more plausible than one that defies everything we know about how the world works and what is possible in it. In the entire history of the world, the correct explanation for any event has never been "magic", or "the laws of physics, chemistry and biology were temporarily suspended by an invisible being in the sky". The difference between the faithful and the skeptic is the quantity and quality of evidence they require in spiritual matters, not how smart they are. In turn, I think that the quantity and quality of evidence one requires depends on what they want to believe, what others close to them believe, and what belief is emotionally gratifying.

We know this much about people with certainty; we are imperfect, as is the process by which we evaluate information and claims. None of us are immune to the imperfections that afflict mankind, though we usually don't see our own. There is an old Mexican saying that the fox doesn't see his own tail. Jesus mentioned that some see a sliver in their neighbor's eye, but not the log in their own. We rarely see our own errors, ignorance and mistakes for what they are and often double down on them using rationalizations and excuses.

Who among us has not seen someone justify their actions after an argument in which they were obviously wrong, and they knew it? Who has not seen a parent justify something their offspring did, or at least make it sound reasonable, when it was clearly wrong? Referee errors in any game are more or less egregious, depending on how they affect the team you are cheering for. In my years of policing, I found that every fight involved at least two people, both of whom could later explain why they were the aggrieved party and righteous in their effort to beat the other guy to a pulp. Most car crashes involved two vehicles and drivers, and each was certain that the other was at fault. Even in a single car crash, I have heard the driver deny any culpability. If we are honest, we have all defended beliefs adamantly, that we later learned were dead wrong. Human nature and our brain's ability to see things correctly haven't changed since Jesus time.

One important thing that has changed since ancient times is our ability to use the scientific method, the best way mankind has found to distinguish claims that are true from those that are false. It is the best way to filter out rationalizations, excuses, and logical fallacies. The scientific method is not a religion as some have claimed, but is the most reliable method yet discovered to separate the wheat from the chaff, fact from fiction, truth from legend. Some have argued against reliance on science, because its answers change. "This food is bad for you", and a few years later, "it's good for you". That's exactly why science is the best course to follow. As new research uncovers new evidence, as mankind's knowledge grows, scientists review it, debate it, and go wherever the evidence leads them, even if it is a new and different course that requires they admit error. The alternative is to follow dogma, legend and old wives tales, which never change, even as the evidence does. There is undeniably some emotional comfort in a consistent, unchanging world. However, if we relied on dogma, legend and old wives tales, we would still be teaching kids that the earth is flat and the center of the universe, which the sun revolves around. We would be sniffing posies to avoid the plague instead of using antibiotics, and using medicine wagon potions instead of modern pharmaceuticals with proven safety and effectiveness. So, let's talk. How does our society effectively work with all the conflicting beliefs and opinions, some of which are wrong, some enlightened, and some thought to be absolute?

In a pluralistic society, we must first find a way to agree on what is factual, so that we can use facts to guide our actions. Facts and evidence alone don't guarantee agreement. Even with all of the facts uncontested, people will differ in how they weigh the relative importance of them. However, without reliance on facts and evidence, changing minds and reaching a reasonable consensus becomes impossible. In 21st century America, discerning what is factual has become more difficult than one might think, for a number of reasons.

One problem I see is that certain news outlets have become little more than propaganda channels for their favored political ideology. In the past, the government, through the FCC, effectively prohibited such monopolies on opinion by enforcing the fairness doctrine. They could broadcast political opinion, but were required to give opposing views equal air time. The deregulation of the Reagan years ended that rule and enabled the development of ideology based news sources. People being what we are, viewers tend to use news sources that confirm what they already believe is true. Such viewers are deprived of a fair analysis of the evidence, or in some instances, even awareness of facts or data that are contrary to beliefs they hold. In such an environment, commentary masquerades as news, and propaganda and half-truths can be put forward as fact, uncontested. Little wonder then that we have become increasingly polarized.

A second problem is that as of 2019, 55% of adults in America get their news often or sometimes, from social media. "Why is that a problem", one might ask. First, you have to understand how social media works. Begin by recognizing that you don't pay anything to get on social media. It's not provided for you free out of the goodness of anyone's heart. It is wise to recognize that if you are not paying for a product, you *are* the product. Advertisers love to target their advertising to the people who are most likely to be receptive. Social media companies track what you like, follow, click on, and how long you look at it. Hopefully you don't think that the personality tests available for free online that purport to tell you what kind of person you are were posted only for your personal edification. They want to know as much about you as they can and develop an algorithm matching people, their preferences, demographics, and the products and services their advertisers provide. Read a post about contrails, and you will get more articles about other, similar conspiracy theories. Thus the articles you read will be skewed and influence your views of reality without your conscious awareness. There are no standards of journalistic integrity on social media. You may remember the 2016 election, when false claims and allegations were rampant on social media, so much so that it was impossible to fact check them as fast as they were being produced. Adding to the confusion, when a meme or story that is a hoax goes viral, it may draw some attention from legitimate news reports, giving it an air of legitimacy. Russia didn't have to do a lot of work to disseminate disinformation; all they had to do was take advantage of the opportunity that was already available to them.

Reinstituting some regulation of public airwaves such as the fairness doctrine may help. Others have been exploring how social media might evolve to lessen the problem of disinformation. Until then, we do well to consider the credibility of a news source, expose ourselves to a variety of news outlets, and resist the tendency to shut out those that present information that may make us uncomfortable. Credibility does not require your agreement.

An educated electorate is crucial for democracy to be successful. Without it, people succumb to foolish analogies and overly simplified solutions to complex problems. For example, a national economy is nothing like running your household budget, though many people think they operate on the same principles. Without critical thinking skills, people often fall prey to logical fallacies, conspiracy theories and simple clichés to solve problems. No societal problem in the history of mankind has ever been solved by following the advice on a bumper sticker. Societies and the people in them are very complex, and solutions to one problem often create new problems. Simple solutions for complex problems don't exist. A fundamental understanding of statistics is needed to critically evaluate data and recognize when the facts are being misrepresented. An educated electorate needs to understand something of economics, marketing, statistics, history, and most importantly, how to think critically and logically. The electorate must know how to evaluate data and evidence to reach a reasonable conclusion and fashion a solution likely to produce the desired outcome. That is a task for public education. While everyone need not be expert, a broad general understanding of these topics among our populace will serve the public interest.

Recent times have produced legislation that I find very disconcerting. The disparity between the level of firearms violence in America and other modern democracies is huge. Yet congress has passed legislation that prohibits the Centers for Disease Control from studying firearms violence, due to concerns about what they would find and how that information might be used. Similarly, when Wisconsin passed concealed carry legislation, the law restricted the information law enforcement agencies could compile, information which could have born directly on the efficacy of the legislation. While there are many valid reasons for limiting access to certain types of data, prohibiting the gathering of data as a matter of law, because it may not be favorable to your cause, is inexcusable. It is legislating willful ignorance. If the evidence does not support your cause, it is your cause that should be re-examined. Information, evidence and data can only help us make better decisions and their collection and analysis should never be prohibited.

Let's also make a distinction between what we know, what we can prove, and what we have simply accepted as true but aren't sure of. Public policy decisions should be made on the basis of facts and evidence, regardless of whether or not they conform to our ideology. When the facts and ideology are in conflict, it is always ideology that should give way.

What of our religious beliefs? How do they fit into a society based on reason and evidence? We must accept everyone's right to believe what they choose, whether it is because they find it comforting, uplifting, enjoy the companionship they receive from like-minded people, weigh the evidence differently than we do, or just believe it is factually the truth. We must also accept that you have no right to require me to live by your unproven beliefs, nor do I have a right to require you to live by mine. In a free society we have every right to live by our own beliefs, as long as they do no harm to others or our greater society. A foundational principle of America, after all, was freedom. That freedom includes both freedom *of* and freedom *from* religion. We must determine what we need to do to live in harmony, and resist efforts to control the thoughts and actions of others that are not necessary to achieve that goal. That becomes easier, once we accept that we are all human, subject to biases in our thinking. We are imperfect, sometimes fragile, sometimes aggressive, and sometimes wrong.

It can be done. This is not an impossible dream. The Amish don't believe people should drive cars, but they don't prohibit everyone else from driving them or try to put automobile manufacturers out of business. Jews believe God commanded you should not eat pork, so they don't; but you can eat all you want without any trouble from them. You are free to follow your own conscience. Islam holds that women must dress modestly, so Muslim women do, but they haven't hired lobbyists to get bikinis outlawed in America. Pastafarians wear colanders in their driver's license photos, but don't insist everyone else must do the same. You get the idea. Live by your faith, whatever it is. Don't impose it on everyone else as a matter of law, at least not until you can objectively prove God is there and what He demands to everyone's satisfaction. Even the Roman Empire let their subjects believe what they wanted about the supernatural, as long as they didn't try to use it to govern or usurp Roman authority. So until you find that proof, let every person be responsible for their own eternal destiny, assuming they have one. Recognize there is a chance, however slight, that it may be you who has the wrong understanding of God's will for our governance. America can only survive in harmony as one nation, by once again respecting the separation of church and state that our founders intended.

For some, it may be incomprehensible that we don't have to be ruled by faith; faith in what heaven commands, or what some men have declared heaven commands. Recent trends have shown that an increasing number of Americans are not committed to particular religious dogma, and when asked their religious preference, report "none".

Often called "Nones" by pollsters and the press, they provide us with hope for the future. How might a nation be ruled without an underlying religious foundation? I submit, much better. We can be ruled by reason and evidence, while guided by compassion and the common good. That future is enlightened and looks much brighter than when we were ruled by faith.